**Protecting Your Privacy and Anonymity
Online: A Guide for Everyone
(Gnu/Linux Edition)**

By Philip Perry

<u>Copyright 2013 by Philip Perry</u>
<u>ALL RIGHTS RESERVED</u>

<u>ISBN 978-1-304-33324-7</u>

This book is a copyrighted work, and I reserve all rights in accordance with the copyright laws of the United States of America. My copyright has been registered with the U.S. Copyright Office; this work was initially published in 2013.

Please note that I understand and respect "fair use" rights, and I won't make any effort to stop you from engaging in activities that fall within "fair use" under the laws of the U.S.A. (Even if your own country doesn't offer such protections).

I have decided to offer a special PDF-only version of the Gnu/Linux edition of <u>Protecting Your Privacy and Anonymity Online</u> as a free download on my website, as a supplement to this work and a free sample. It comes with fairly liberal permissions, so be sure to check it out.

You can find the free PDF-only version of this book here:
<u>http://tech-hermitage.com/PrivacyAndAnonymity/</u>

*This book has been written
with much appreciation for
whistleblowers who show us what
our government is up to and
hackers who give us technology
we can use to counter it.*

Keep up the good work, guys.

<u>One Small But Important Disclaimer:</u>

The information in this book is provided in the hope that it will be useful to you and help you preserve some of your privacy and anonymity in spite of all the efforts going on to take it away from you. My goal is to share information about some great software and some alternative ways of doing things which I believe will make you much safer, even though they might not protect you entirely (nothing can protect you entirely).

Please note that I am providing this information in the hope that it will be useful, but <u>with no warranty whatsoever.</u> Should you read this book and/or use the information provided in it, you agree that <u>you are doing so at your own risk</u>, <u>you fully indemnify me against all claims</u>, and <u>you hold me harmless in all matters related to your use of this information.</u>

Table of Contents:

Chapter #	**Description**	**Page #**
0	Preface	i
1	Why You Should be Concerned About Your Privacy and Anonymity.	1
2	Remain Private and Anonymous On the Web With the Onion Router and Its Tor-Enabled Browser.	11
3	How to Protect Your Private Files Using the Gnu Privacy Guard and Strong Encryption, and Encrypt Files to Send to Others.	37
4	Encrypting Your Email With Thunderbird and Enigmail.	71
5	Instant Messaging.	97
6	Afterword	119

Preface:

Originally, I tried to write something deep here, something that would convey how pissed off and dismayed I was that my government had gone full Stasi, collecting everything everyone did online, everyone's telephone metadata, etc... I did my best, but I'm not really good at that kind of thing; when I read it back later, and asked myself "what would I think if I wasn't me" the only thing that came to mind is "My God, this is boring... when is he going to get to the point?". It read like a long shaggy dog story. So I erased all of it and started again.

Straight to the point, then: The U.S. government has decided that it's a good idea to become the modern equivalent of George Orwell's "Big Brother". They're building the biggest, most arrogant surveillance apparatus that has ever been attempted, they're lying about it daily in the news, and the worldview they display when they talk about it makes it clear they think what they're doing is not only acceptable, but necessary and patriotic. Of course, most regular citizens disagree rather strongly, but the government only pretends to listen, while planning how to spin whatever phony reform they eventually try to appease us with.

Some people argue that *only* the government can take action. They claim that there is no technological solution, that nobody can do *anything* about the NSA snooping on everyone because *government agencies are so omniscient and all-powerful that the best we can do is beg Congress to intervene on our behalf.* These people bug me; they're so fatalistic. It's as if they think should all just throw our hands in the air and give up, begging Congress to fix the mess that *Congress started in the first place.* Why should we belive they'll do any such thing? *They have absolutely no desire to change anything whatsoever about the situation.* Things are exactly the way Congress and the President wanted them to be, and this is how they want things to remain. **The only thing we as individuals can do is adapt to the situation and do what we can to take our privacy back for ourselves (insofar as such a thing is possible).**

There *are* some things we can do. *We're not entirely powerless.* Technical people all over the world are doing everything they can to sort this mess out, whether the government wants them to or not. Now that the surveillance state the government has been assembling has become common knowledge, people are empowering themselves to opt out of it. You can, too. This book will get you started, it'll give you some good ideas on where you can begin.

But, let me warn you in advance, although the software you'll read about in this book is very good, and will help you significantly towards achieving privacy and anonymity online and off, *you must remember that no software is perfect*. If someone powerful enough takes an interest in you, all the software in the world won't keep him from sticking his nose into everything you do. Also, you have to be very careful if you want to be anonymous and private online. All it takes is one mistake, and you're revealed. You have to pay attention to what you're doing, and you have to try really hard not to slip up. Having said that, *if you don't try to preserve your privacy, it'll be gone anyway*. It's worthwhile to at least try, isn't it?

This brings us to Gnu/Linux, and the Free Software movement. I think Gnu/Linux (and Free Software in general) offer the best, most powerful tools available to protect your privacy and anonymity. No proprietary system can even come close; in fact, proprietary systems are inherently untrustworthy because they're owned by corporations, which governments can bend to their will and silence with gag orders.

I think Gnu/Linux' open-source and multinational nature make it somewhat immune to government interference. Here's why: every time some organization releases a new version of Gnu/Linux, they also release the full source code. Thousands of people around the world immediately download this source code and start fooling around with it. Maybe they just compile it and compare the checksums of their binaries against the ones on the organization's download page. Maybe they actually read the source code, looking for bugs. If some foolish government managed to get a backdoor inserted into a version of Linux, their code would be discovered, possibly within hours, and the entire world would laugh at them. Then their backdoor would be patched out of existence. It would be humiliating! For this reason alone, I don't think they'd dare trying to hack an entire distribution. Logically, I think the only thing they could get away with would be targeting a specific individual and trying to trick him into installing a poisoned Gnu/Linux on one of his systems. Even this would be of limited utility; the person could just download a new copy of Gnu/Linux and reinstall.

Some Thoughts About Gnu/Linux:

I have an enormous amount of respect and affection for Gnu/Linux; I've been using it since 1995. Since then, I've run Red Hat Linux, Red Hat's free Fedora Project, OpenSUSE, Slackware, Mandrake, Kubuntu, and Ubuntu, not to mention Gnu/Linux's cousins FreeBSD, OpenBSD, and NetBSD. Of these, my favorite is Fedora. It offers a number of things of interest to people who like their privacy:

1. Fedora doesn't include any non-free software, so everything that comes with the system is open source. This means there are a lot of people (hackers, security professionals, developers, interested users) looking at all its components' source code on a regular basis. It's extremely difficult if not impossible for any government agency to inject any backdoors in such a system and get away with it.
2. Fedora offers great support for encryption, and its repositories offer all of the tools I'm

going to recommend to you in this book. The only thing you're going to have to download is the Tor Browser package; this is available in the repositories as well, but it's nice to be able to download Tor into a single directory you can delete in a hurry if you have to.
3. Fedora lets you encrypt your entire hard drive, including the operating system itself. This is magnificent for privacy, because it makes it completely impossible for anyone to tamper with your system when you're not around. Of course, you have to remember to turn your PC off when you're not using it!
4. Fedora also offers built-in support for SELinux ("Security Enhanced Linux"), which was originally developed by the NSA to protect their computers. Microsoft sued to make them stop contributing, claiming that it represented unfair government assistance to one of Microsoft's competitors, and the project was released to the open source community, which has managed it ever since. SELinux significantly improves the security of your system.

To get Fedora, just go to their website. Instead of downloading the Live CD, download the installation DVD, because this gives you everything (which is more convenient). Here's the URL you'll want to access: https://fedoraproject.org/

Fedora is truly a wonderful operating system. It's just about the most secure system available to us ordinary people, and if you use its better features (like full disk encryption) you can enjoy a level of security unparallelled in the proprietary software world.

One more thing:

Thank you for buying this paper copy. By doing so, you've directly helped me, and I want you to know how much I appreciate it. It means a lot to me.

Every now and then, please check the website where I keep the free PDF version of this book. You should pick up a copy of the free PDF for your cell phone and laptop. Please accept it with my compliments. As I issue corrected or new versions of this book, they'll be released in the PDF first, so you can get updates there.

Philip Perry,
In the Adirondacks,
01/07/2014

Updated 6/14/2014

Supplemental Note, added 7/26/2013: Fedora has a wonderful tool, found in the KDE menu in Applications/System, called "Fedora LiveUSB Creator". Everything in this book can ALSO be done from within a LiveUSB install, meaning you can put a Fedora system on a USB thumbdrive, boot to it and add all the good stuff we'll be talking about. Then, you can do all your anonymous stuff while booted into that, leaving no trace whatsoever of your web browsing on your actual laptop.

Even better, you can download an iso for a Gnu/Linux-based operating system called "Tails" which comes with many of the tools in this book already installed. You can use the LiveUSB creator to put Tails on a thumbdrive and be ready to go in minutes. If you really want to get fancy, you can get yourself a cheap laptop on Craigslist, pull the hard drive so it has no permanent storage at all, and use tails with that.

See what I mean about Gnu/Linux-based tools being the best? Try and put a proprietary O/S on a thumbdrive... Not happening. For anonymity, Gnu/Linux is definitely the way to go. It's like voodoo!

Chapter 1:

Why You Should be Concerned About Your Privacy and Anonymity

This chapter is going to present four arguments condemning corporate and governmental attempts to eliminate privacy and anonymity, so you can see why I think it's so important for us to protect both. If you already agree with me that corporations and the government should respect our constitutional rights and stop spying on us, you can skip this chapter and jump into the good stuff. However, if you're still on the fence about whether you should be worried about government and corporate surveillance, please read this chapter and keep an open mind. Before we begin, let's look at what *my* government has been up to lately.

You're Not Paranoid: They Really ARE Spying On You

I'm sure you've heard about the former NSA contractor turned whistleblower Edward Snowden and his leak of documents to the Guardian, a British newspaper. Thanks to him, we've learned that the NSA is able to capture virtually anything that anyone does online, via both direct Internet backbone connections and site-specific connections provided by large companies. We've learned that they were forcing phone companies like Verizon and AT&T to hand over cell phone metadata for millions of users, and using this data to try and figure out who has been associating with people the NSA was interested in. Similarly, we've learned that the government has been collecting email metadata since 2001, and has collected something like 20 trillion metadata records for analysis. The government claims they care about our privacy and our rights, and their critics say they're just trying to put a positive spin on things. I'm obviously with the critics on this, but even if I trusted my government it wouldn't matter. They don't seem to understand that *all future administrations will inherit the surveillance powers the current government is creating*, and *we don't know what they're going to do with them*. Let's look at a couple of the programs we've heard about.

The following information came from the Guardian's series on NSA surveillance. You can find it at this URL:

http://www.guardian.co.uk/world/nsa

The two programs that are currently getting the most attention are the NSA's PRISM and Upstream programs. Within Upstream, we learned about FAIRVIEW and BLARNEY.

PRISM is a system whereby the government can collect data from large technology companies as long as the NSA have FISA court approval (which is little more than a rubber stamp, giving the NSA anything it asks for). Mr. Snowden's leaked powerpoint slides named Microsoft, Yahoo, Google, Facebook, Paltalk, YouTube, AOL, Skype, and Apple as participants, and claimed that the data could be collected "directly from the company's servers". These companies immediately denied that the government had any such direct access, and one theory I've seen in a few articles on the subject was that the powerpoint author exaggerated what was really going on. Perhaps, for instance, there was an FTP site or drop box provided by each company allowing the NSA to retrieve their information requests. This would be on a company owned server, and in a sense, "direct". Google has asked the government to allow it to explain to their customers what they've been compelled to provide and how, so perhaps one day it'll be more clear. In any case, PRISM somehow, in some poorly explained and secretive way, allows the NSA to collect data from these companies, and all they need is FISA approval (which is almost always granted).

According to one of Mr. Snowden's leaked slides, PRISM is able to collect email, chat (video and voice), videos, photos, stored data, VOIP, file transfers, video conferencing, your login activity, and your social networking details. That's basically everything, all without a warrant or probable cause.

Here's the Washington Post's collection of material on PRISM:
http://www.washingtonpost.com/wp-srv/special/politics/prism-collection-documents/

Upstream is a set of government programs that collect data directly from the Internet's backbone fiber optic lines. According to Mark Klein, a former AT&T technician who originally exposed the existence of this capability in 2006, a beam splitter is used to send an exact copy of all traffic passing through the Internet's fiber optic lines into locked rooms at telecom facilities where the data can be captured by the NSA. The room he exposed, "Room 641A" at SBC Communications in San Francisco, was the subject of a Frontline episode in May, 2007, and also mentioned in the Nova episode "The Spy Factory". A recent article in Wired Magazine about the NSA's new Utah data center theorized that the NSA is running 10 to 20 facilities like Room 641A across the U.S. (the article referred to them as "Domestic Listening Posts"). *The same article quoted an NSA whistleblower as saying that if the NSA only wanted to capture international traffic, they would have placed their listening posts on the points where Internet lines entered the country, but they tapped backbone switches throughout the U.S instead, enabling them to spy on domestic traffic as well.*

You should read the Wired article; you can find it here:
http://www.wired.com/threatlevel/2012/03/ff_nsadatacenter/

The Nova episode "The Spy Factory" can be watched here:
http://www.pbs.org/wgbh/nova/military/spy-factory.html

If you want to watch numerous articles on YouTube about Room 641A, use the following two searches:
http://www.youtube.com/results?search_query=NSA+Room+641a
http://www.youtube.com/results?search_query=Mark+Klein+NSA

The BLARNEY program is part of Upstream, and collects internet metadata directly from these fiber optic lines. Metadata is data about communications: who is communicating with whom, when, and where. It's used in the same way cell phone metadata is used: to figure out who is associating with whom, and learn about our friends, family, and work associates. This may seem innocuous, but it's not at all. I'll explain how this hurts you, and how it hurts society, a little later on. Where BLARNEY concentrates on metadata, FAIRVIEW seems to be the international counterpart to the PRISM program, involving deals with foreign telecom companies to allow the NSA to pull data directly from their fiber optic lines.

Here's a good Guardian article about FAIRVIEW in Brazil:
http://www.guardian.co.uk/commentisfree/2013/jul/07/nsa-brazilians-globo-spying

So, put all of this together, and what do you have? Under PRISM, the NSA can force major American Internet companies to hand over your data wholesale, bypassing the fourth and fifth amendments using secret FISA court orders. Under the Upstream programs, whatever the NSA can't get directly from Internet companies they can just grab directly from the fiber optic lines that make up the Internet backbone, again, bypassing your fourth and fifth amendment rights. They've got programs that grab metadata and programs that collect data, programs for domestic data and programs for international data. It's quite amazing, and it was all constructed in complete secrecy.

This level of surveillance involves capturing and storing a vast amount of data. The NSA is busily constructing a gigantic data center in Utah to do just that. Don't take my word for it; you can read about it in the Wired article I mentioned earlier, "The NSA Is Building the Country's Biggest Spy Center (Watch What You Say)". Again, you can find it here:

http://www.wired.com/threatlevel/2012/03/ff_nsadatacenter/.

Now that you have an idea of what the U.S. government has been getting up to, let me present you with my arguments about why you should be horrified by it, or at least extremely suspicious about it, and by extension, why you should want to protect your privacy and anonymity from the government and corporations who want to take it away.

Argument #1: The Government Can't Be Trusted With This Kind of Power

The programs I've mentioned here are only the ones that have been revealed to us; there's probably quite a bit more we don't know about yet. The government says we should trust them, that their targets are supposed to be non-citizens (as if that makes it alright) and that they don't misuse any of our data that they "inadvertently" collect. But we *shouldn't* trust them; in fact, blindly trusting the government is not only breathtakingly naive, it's downright un-American.

Our entire form of government is based on the idea that governments are inherently untrustworthy, that power tends to corrupt and must be limited. Limiting the power of our government is one of the most important functions of our Constitution. It's the reason the government was broken into thirds, the executive, legislative, and judicial branches. The idea is that no one branch can ever usurp power while the other two are looking over its shoulder.

History has shown us that the founders were right: *the government can't be trusted*. In fact, the U.S. has a long history of mistreating and spying on its citizens. Here are a few notable examples:

In 1947, the House Un-American Activities Committee conducted hearings in which prominent members of the entertainment industry were interrogated about their connections to the communist party. Those who refused to answer or refused to testify against their colleagues were jailed for contempt of Congress and placed on the infamous "Hollywood Blacklist". This meant the end of their careers; those who couldn't go underground or leave the U.S. were unable to work in the industry. The blacklist was in effect from 1947 through 1960, when it was finally broken. In the end over 300 people saw their careers destroyed.

During the Second Red Scare (1950-1956), Senator Joseph McCarthy carried out a witch hunt against communists, claiming that they had infiltrated our government, our unions, and the entertainment industry. Suspicions were investigated aggressively, and people were often presumed guilty with little evidence against them. The FBI was used extensively in these investigations.

Interestingly, President Truman compared J. Edgar Hoover's FBI to the Gestapo, and argued that it was turning into a form of "secret police". He accused Hoover's FBI of engaging in blackmail, and claimed that Congress was afraid of both the FBI and Hoover himself. Hoover's FBI was known to use its surveillance powers to smear the reputations of innocent citizens and pressure politicians to go along with Hoover's goals.

The most infamous program of Hoover's FBI was called "COINTELPRO". This used spies, informants, and agents provocateurs to disrupt and spy on any organization Hoover considered subversive. Initially it focused on communists during the Second Red Scare and eventually targeted a wide variety of citizens including civil rights activists and hippies. The program was in operation from 1956 to 1971, when it was investigated by Congress and declared illegal and unconstitutional by the Church Committee. Two notable people the FBI conducted intense surveillance on during this period were Dr. Martin Luther King and Malcolm X. Both men were assassinated, and in each case the FBI was suspected of involvement in their deaths.

In 1972, not so long after the Church Committee condemned COINTELPRO, President Nixon resigned from office to avoid being impeached. He had tried to use former CIA employees to bug the Democratic National Committee headquarters at the Watergate hotel, but they got caught in the act. Worse, he tried to use the CIA to pressure the FBI to cover the whole thing up.

The 1980s brought us Iran-Contra, and the CIA's involvement in the Central American drug trade. The 1990's brought the FBI/ATF sieges at Ruby Ridge, Idaho and Waco, Texas, both of which involved a heavy-handed, brutal approach that resulted in unnecessary bloodshed. We also saw the FBI's first attempts to monitor the Internet and email, with programs like Carnivore (an email capture system).

After 9/11, the Bush/Cheney administration began using so-called "extraordinary rendition" (i.e. kidnapping, and transport in rented private aircraft) to bypass due process and carry suspected terrorists off to "black sites" (CIA-run prisons in foreign countries which practice torture). They suspended habeas corpus for non-citizens (calling them "illegal enemy combatants"), imprisoning them indefinitely without trial and torturing them, sometimes for years. They attempted to do this to U.S. citizens as well and only failed because in Hamdi v. Rumsfeld, the Supreme Court ruled that habeas corpus could not be suspended for a U.S. citizen.

Under Bush/Cheney, we saw the creation of the Department of Homeland Security; the formation of so-called "immigration checkpoints" up to a hundred miles inside U.S. borders; the creation of the Transportation Security Administration and related insane levels of airport security; and secret "no fly" lists of people who were not permitted to use air travel. The no-fly lists are notorious for "false positives" and for being used vindictively against protestors and activists. Despite promises of "Hope and Change" from President Obama, all these creations of the Bush administration still exist and are regularly being used against Americans.

More recently, we've had numerous cases where Federal prosecutors used plea bargaining practices to hound relatively harmless people into accepting years in prison for crimes that should have been treated as misdemeanors. The system has been set up so a prosecutor can threaten to demand the maximum possible sentences for numerous trumped-up "crimes", all to be served consecutively, unless a suspect (often innocent!) agrees to plead guilty to some lesser crime and spend years in prison. This is a direct attack against our right to a jury trial, and it supports a massive, cruel prison industry which uses prisoners as de-facto slave labor. Prisons are increasingly being privatized as well, which creates a profit motive for incarcertating as many people as possible.

Argument #2: There Aren't Any Strong Protections In These NSA Programs; They're Likely to be Misused

The government claims that there are strong protections built into their domestic spying programs. They say we shouldn't worry about the surveillance state, because they care about our constitutional rights and have built safeguards into their programs to make sure our rights are protected. Unfortunately, these claims are misleading. Congress has given the NSA numerous legal loopholes to allow them to use an American's data or share it with other intelligence agencies, bypassing the fourth and fifth amendments.

For example, if they believe they've found evidence of a crime (or even that someone might be about to commit one) they can share your data with the FBI, ignoring the fourth amendment entirely. If they can't read your data because it's encrypted, they can keep it in hope that they'll be able to read it later. If they can't be sure you're within the boundaries of the United States, or if they think you're communicating with someone outside the country, they can keep it. If they think your data has any value to their intelligence efforts, they can keep it. All of these decisions are made by the NSA analysts themselves, and according to Mr. Snowden, they're told that they should assume they'll be given the "benefit of the doubt" and that they shouldn't worry if they accidentally grab an American's data. There's really nothing preventing your data from being misused, or used against you. It's all subjective, giving the NSA all the "wiggle room" it needs.

Technically, the director of the NSA should have to sign off on intra-agency requests, and on requests to use an American's data. I doubt he'd hesitate to sign off on *any* requests presented to him, so this is a very weak protection. Also, although this is the NSA's current policy, Congress and the FISA court could change the rules at any time.

Argument #3: Mass Surveillance Is Unconstitutional, and Harms Society

I believe that applying this sort of mass surveillance to virtually everybody is almost certainly unconstitutional. I believe it flagrantly violates our fourth and fifth amendment rights, and significantly weakens our first amendment rights in an indirect way.

Here's what the fourth amendment to the Constitution says:

> *IV. The right of the people to be secure in their persons, houses, papers, and effects, against unreasonable searches and seizures, shall not be violated, and no Warrants shall issue, but upon probable cause, supported by Oath or affirmation, and particularly describing the place to be searched, and the persons or things to be seized.*

The Internet didn't exist in the 1700s, but its equivalent at the time was your "papers": your personal records, your correspondence with other people, in other words, your information. The modern Internet is just another way for you to communicate and share information (i.e. papers), and therefore it isn't a magical "Constitution free zone" no matter how badly the government might like it to be.

Let's look more closely at the amendment. We have the right to be secure in our persons, houses, papers and effects from unreasonable searches and seizures. No warrants can be issued (i.e. no searches may be made) unless the government can show probable cause, supported by someone making an oath or affirmation, and the warrants must describe exactly what the government will be looking for. *Capturing everything and searching through it all in case any of it is of interest to the NSA or FBI is an absolute violation of our fourth amendment rights!*

Now let's look at the fifth amendment. The fifth amendment says:

> ***V. No person shall be held to answer for a capital, or otherwise infamous crime, unless on a presentment or indictment of a Grand Jury, except in cases arising in the land or naval forces, or in the Militia, when in actual service in time of War or public danger; nor shall any person be subject for the same offense to be twice put in jeopardy of life or limb; <u>nor shall be compelled in any criminal case to be a witness against himself, nor be deprived of life, liberty, or property, without due process of law; nor shall private property be taken for public use, without just compensation</u>.***

Consider the underlined portions. The government can't make you act as a witness against yourself (but they want to read all your private communications in case there's anything they can use against you). They can't deprive you of life, liberty, or property without due process of law (but they think it's OK to acquire and copy all your private communications without a warrant or probable cause in case they might want to use them against you). And they can't take private property without just compensation (but they think it's perfectly OK to search through all your private communications and the related metadata, *information that has value,* without giving you a nickel). I think they're violating the fifth amendment, too.

Now let's consider how these surveillance programs are harming several of our most important basic human rights, the ones detailed in the very first amendment to the Constitution. Here's the text, for your reading pleasure:

> ***I. Congress shall make no law respecting an establishment of religion, or prohibiting the free exercise thereof; or abridging the freedom of speech, or of the press; or the right of the people peaceably to assemble, and to petition the Government for a redress of grievances.***

Widespread warrantless surveillance abridges our freedom of speech and of the press, it definitely attacks the right of the people to peacefully assemble, and it makes it a whole lot harder to petition the government for redress of grievances. It even attacks our freedom of religion. Here's how.

First, it attacks your freedom of speech. Since you know that everything you say online might be recorded and used against you, you'll naturally censor yourself. If saying the wrong thing can get you branded a subversive, or cause the government to investigate you and everyone you know, you'll be too afraid to speak your mind. If you have any controversial points of view, you'll be likely to keep them to yourself. Lawyers like to call this a "chilling effect".

Second, it attacks freedom of the press by making people afraid to talk to reporters, and making reporters afraid to investigate controversial subjects. How can you protect the confidentiality of your sources if the government is listening to all your communications and tracking your cell phone metadata? Again, if saying the wrong thing can invite retaliation from the government, you're going to self-censor even if you're a member of the press.

Third, it attacks your freedom to peacefully assemble. When the government is using cell phone metadata to identify all the friends and family of a target and investigate or harass them as well, people become afraid to associate with anyone that might draw the government's attention. It gives the government the power to stigmatize dissenters, to create instant pariahs of people they don't approve of. "Don't talk to protestors or the government's going to investigate you!" It's subtle, but terrible.

There's another way in which the surveillance state attacks your right to peacefully assemble. You may not have heard about this, but here in the U.S, there's a thing called the "no fly list". You can't find out if you're on it, because it's a secret. You can't find out how you got on it, because that's also a secret. You can't easily get off it, either, because there's no way to challenge how you got on it in the first place. During the Bush administration, activists were often put on the no-fly list to prevent them from participating in rallies and protests. If you spoke out against the administration, they would use the no-fly list to punish you. With the NSA recording virtually everything that everyone says online, all it takes is one forum comment and one annoyed bureaucrat and you're banned from flying. If you're lucky, all they'll do to you is mark you for unpleasant special attention in the airport security lines.

Finally, it obviously attacks our freedom of religion. Islamic people, for example, tend to capture the government's attention much more than, say, Jewish or Christian people do. If you know that practicing your religion might get the government to investigate you, you'll be afraid to practice your religion openly, or even discuss it. On this particular topic, it's not just the government you have to worry about. There are an awful lot of extremists here in the U.S, people who are all too willing to hate and attack people they consider to be different from themselves. Anonymity and privacy can protect you from such creatures. We'll discuss that in a later chapter.

Argument #4: The Surveillance State Endangers Us All

Consider the current administration for a moment. They don't seem to be using their vast surveillance powers for anything too terrible just yet. Right now, they're just listening, and increasing their surveillance capabilities. Most people aren't even that worried about them, because nothing they're doing is affecting very many people in any obvious way, at least not yet. The current administration isn't *that* bad, after all.

But what about future presidents? We don't know who'll be elected next time, or the time after that. Can you be sure that some future administration won't decide to start persecuting people like you or me? It doesn't matter what your issues are; you could be pro-choice, pro-life, for gun control or a stalwart defender of the second amendment. It doesn't matter if you're a dyed-in-the-wool hippie or a wool-suited company man. Some future administration will disagree with you on some issue sooner or later, and may use these powers to oppress you. It's only a matter of time before someone ends up in office that abuses the vast powers the current president is allowing the NSA to develop and extend.

I think this is the main thing most of my fellow Americans are missing: every time we elect a new president, there's a risk that everything will change in some horrible and unpredictable way. The people who are considered mainstream and normal under one president might be considered enemies of the state by the next. I'm pretty sure Germans in 1933 had no idea what was about to happen. Similarly, Russians under the Czar had no idea what Stalin was going to get up to later on. If Cambodians knew that Pol Pot was going to murder every single intellectual in the country (even killing people who merely wore glasses because they *might* be intellectuals) they probably would have gotten out of there as fast as their legs could carry them. We don't know what's going to happen in the future either, and this constant surveillance puts us all in danger. It gives some future despot a one-stop, full-service search tool to locate and eliminate anyone he considers "subversive".

There's a famous quote by Cardinal Richelieu, the chief minister of the French king Louis XIII: "*If you give me six lines written by the hand of the most honest of men, I will find something in them which will hang him.*" The NSA is creating a system capable of collecting everything any of us ever write, providing future governments with as much material about us as they will ever need. This should frighten you. It certainly frightens me.

In Closing

I've presented a lot of arguments here. I've tried to convince you that you shouldn't trust your government, that in fact it's un-American to trust them. I've shown you examples of how the government has abused its citizens in the past, so you can see there's no reason to assume it won't continue to do so in the future. I've tried to show you that the government is completely ignoring your constitutional rights and that this surveillance is not just wrong, but dangerous.

I don't think for a minute that Congress is able or willing to do anything about the problem. Most of them are too old, too authoritarian, and too wealthy to care. Even if they *did* care, and they *did* so something, *our intelligence agencies are too arrogant -- they'd "work around the problem" by renaming and concealing their programs, and trying harder to prevent whistleblowing.* It's my opinion that the only thing that will help is if we, as individuals, use technology to render the government's surveillance apparatus ineffective (*or at least, less effective*). This book is my contribution, although a small one.

I hope the arguments I've presented in this chapter have convinced you that protecting your privacy and anonymity is a good idea. If you've read everything I've written and you still think the development of an American surveillance state doesn't affect you, then I understand, and I wish you the best of luck. However, if you agree with me that the surveillance state is frightening, and that you would like to learn more about how to hide yourself from it, then please continue to read my book. The tools I'm going to tell you about are pretty good, and not too hard to use. None of them cost any money, and all you'll have to do is spend a little bit of your time. Isn't your privacy worth at least that?

Once again, I must warn you that even with these very good tools, you're never going to be completely immune to government and corporate surveillance. The government and corporations are *always* trying to find new ways to snoop on all of us. They can't help themselves; it's in their nature. So be careful about what you do online, knowing that there's always a risk, even if you take precautions. These tools will make you much safer and more secure, but remember -- it's impossible to be 100% safe or secure. So please be careful.

Chapter 2:

***Remain Private and Anonymous On the Web With
the Onion Router ("Tor") and Its Tor-Enabled Browser***

The most important freedom of all is freedom of speech; without the ability to speak freely without fear of reprisal, we're completely powerless. Worse than that, we become consumers of content rather than producers of it -- we become spectators rather than participants. One of the things I suspect our government is trying to accomplish with their surveillance programs is making us afraid to express ourselves. If we're always looking over our shoulder for the NSA, wondering whether something we post in an online forum is going to get us into trouble, then we're going to censor ourselves. That prevents us from questioning the government, and isolates us from other people who might have agreed with us, people who might have helped us pressure the government to change their policies.

Luckily, we don't have to self-censor. We can choose to be anonymous online, and say whatever we want when and where we want to say it, knowing that nobody can come after us, or shame us, or otherwise persecute us. You'll be surprised how easy it is to do this. If you follow the instructions in this chapter, you can be up and running in ten minutes flat. We'll also talk about some useful things you can do once you're able to be anonymous online.

Everything starts with a wonderful tool called "The Onion Router," or Tor. Tor was invented by the U.S. Naval Research Laboratory to protect government employees from being eavesdropped on or identified while they accessed the Internet overseas. It works via a network of Tor nodes, each of which is like a layer in an onion. You connect to Tor via an "entry node", and as you browse the web your data bounces from Tor node to Tor node until eventually it's sent on to the website you're trying to read through an "exit node". Then, the website's response returns through Tor along a reverse path, bouncing from node to node until it comes back to you.

While using Tor, the website you're connecting to can't tell what your actual IP address is. They can only see the IP address of the Tor exit node they're connected to. Similarly, your ISP can't see the website you're connecting to, because all they see is the Tor entry node you've connected to.

This is what makes Tor such a good way to maintain your anonymity. It prevents anyone from associating your current IP address (assigned by your ISP) with whatever you've been doing online. In other words, it separates you from your activity; it conceals the origin of your forum posts. All anyone can tell is that someone posted something using Tor. At most, they might be able to notice that you were using Tor at the same time the comment was posted, which doesn't prove anything at all.

A few years ago while I was working at the N.Y. State Board of Elections, someone began insulting a politician online. I don't remember exactly what was said, and honestly I didn't care (politicians didn't interest me). But he was apparently some kind of bigshot, and the people in charge of the agency wanted to catch the person pestering him. Our agency's in-house investigator (now retired) came to me in the I.T. unit and asked me to help prove that some guy they suspected was actually responsible for the posts. Note that they thought they knew who the guy was; they just wanted to prove it was actually him. This should have been relatively easy to do. Traditionally, we'd subpoena the web server logs of the forums he was commenting on, then get his ISP to confirm that the IP addresses from the server logs were allocated to him at the time the comments were posted.

Unfortunately for us, it turned out the person was using Tor, and as a result we were completely unable to tie the IP addresses of his forum posts to him. The best we could show was that he was online at approximately the same time as the forum post was made. This was in early evening, when almost *everyone* was online checking email, so it was completely useless. How could anyone prove it wasn't just a coincidence? Millions of people were online at the time. The posts could have been made by anyone. They gave up on the investigation.

There are two morals to this story. First, *Tor works*. Next, if you make sure you do your browsing during peak hours, nobody will be able to match up the times you were online with the time you enjoyed your right to free speech and consider it any more than a coincidence. *So you'll want to do your anonymous browsing during the day or in early evening, not the middle of the night.*

Actually, this brings up a point you should keep in mind whenever you want to remain anonymous online: the old saying about "safety in numbers" is absolutely true. Go online when everyone else is going online, and you become a needle in a haystack. Look like everyone else, and you become invisible.

In order to try Tor for yourself, you'll want to visit the Tor website, at:

https://www.torproject.org/

The site looks like the first image on the next page. You'll want to browse around the main page, particularly reading the "About Tor" section (the history is interesting, and they talk about the various groups that are safely using Tor around the world) and the advice they offer about the ways in which you should change your web browsing habits.

Note that I'm recommending you get Tor from the Tor website rather than Fedora's software repository. There are three reasons for this:

1. The version you get from the Tor website will always be more recent, and more secure, than one you get from a software repository. This is because things take time to find their way into software repositories. Usually this isn't an issue, but when it comes to Tor, you want to update it regularly; your anonymity depends on it.
2. By downloading Tor, you'll have a complete Tor installation with Tor Browser in a single directory on your PC. If you ever have to get rid of it in a hurry (like, say, a bunch of goons are trying to break your door down because they think you've offended someone powerful online), all you have to do is delete it. You can also back it up, complete with all your settings and Tor-only bookmarks, and carry it around on a thumbdrive, plugging in the drive whenever you need some anonymity.

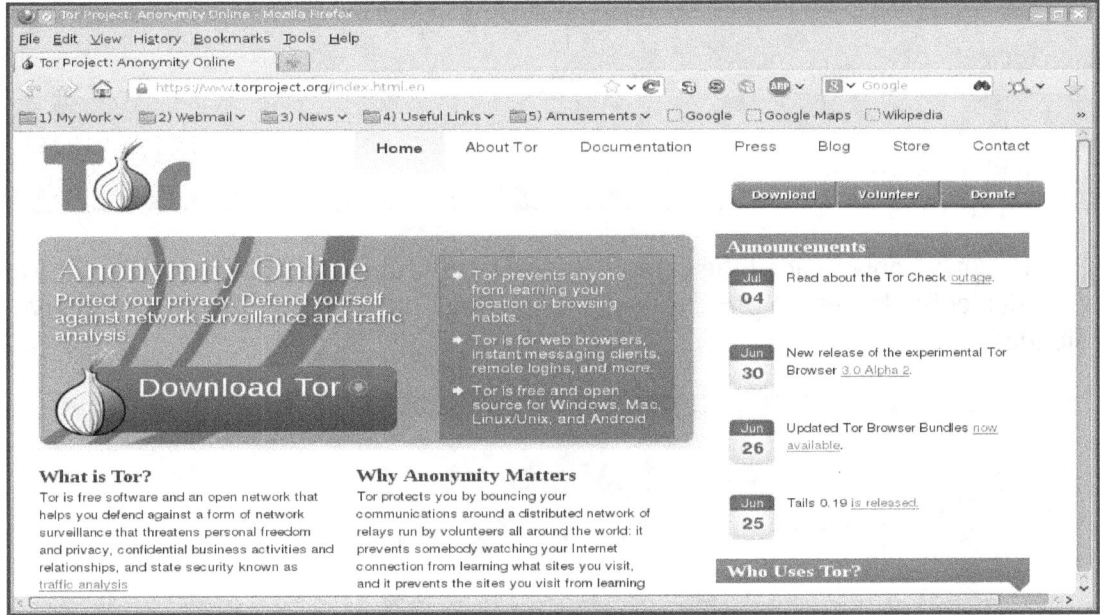

Clicking the download link takes you to a download page for your operating system (in this case, Gnu/Linux). Here, you'll see another download link (as in the image on the next page). Click that to save the Tor install file to your downloads folder. Note that this is not a normal install program; it's just a compressed zip file, ready to be extracted.

The installation page starts up at the top with the proprietary O/S installers; you have to scroll down to find Gnu/Linux. Since I've got 64-bit Fedora 18, I'm going to go for a 64-bit Gnu/Linux install, as you can see here. Click the giant orange button to download a tar.gz file.

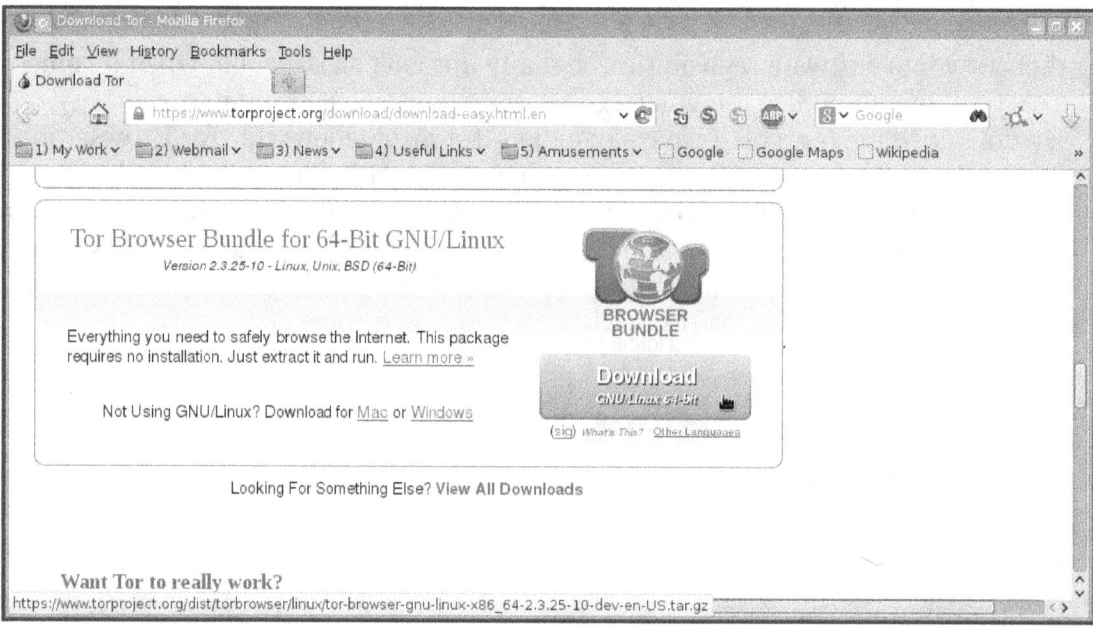

Once you've downloaded the compressed file, right-click it, then click "Extract Archive Here, Autodetect Subfolder" in order to begin extracting Tor. The next image should give you the basic idea.

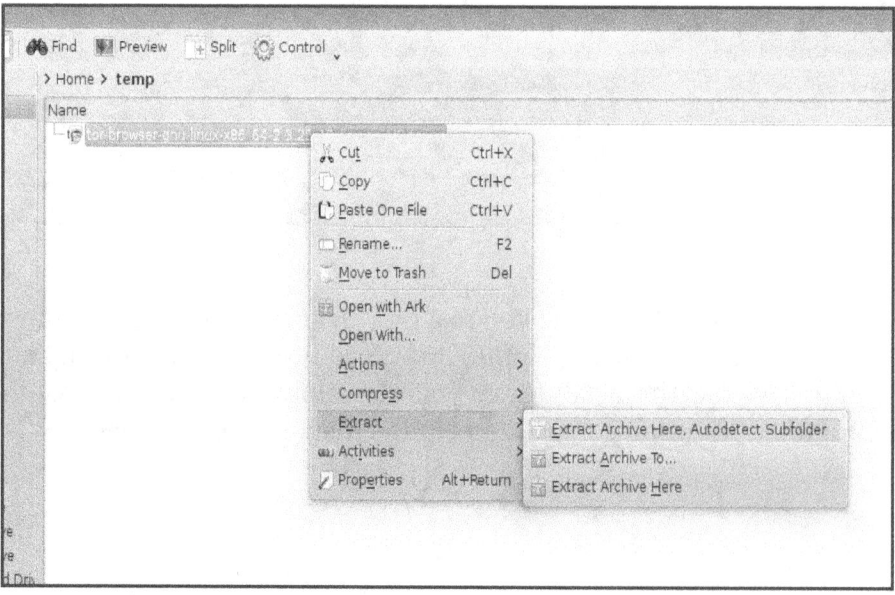

When the process is complete, you'll see an extracted folder which contains a "Tor Browser_en-US" folder containing everything you need to run Tor. In the following image, I've highlighted it. You can move this folder anywhere you want, like for example your main home directory. It's completely self-contained. I like to move it to my home directory and delete the folder that was wrapped around it ("tor-browser-gnu-linux-x86_64-2.3.25.10-dev-en-US"). This keeps things nice and simple. I like to keep the original tar.gz file in case I ever want to reinstall Tor, or give it to someone else. I generally put files like this in an "installfiles" directory in my home directory for safekeeping.

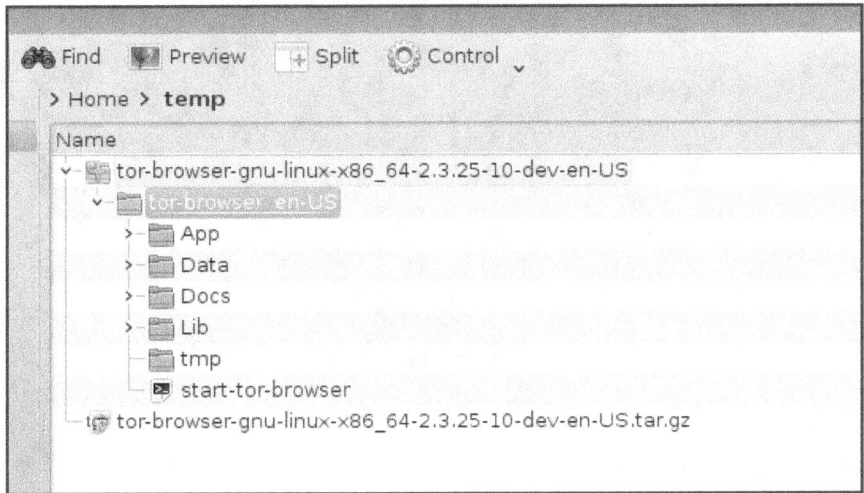

Double click the folder to enter it. You'll see the actual Tor browser program, and a bunch of folders that come with it. All you're concerned with is the browser itself. The next image shows what the contents of the Tor folder should look like; the shell script you should double-click to start Tor is highlighted.

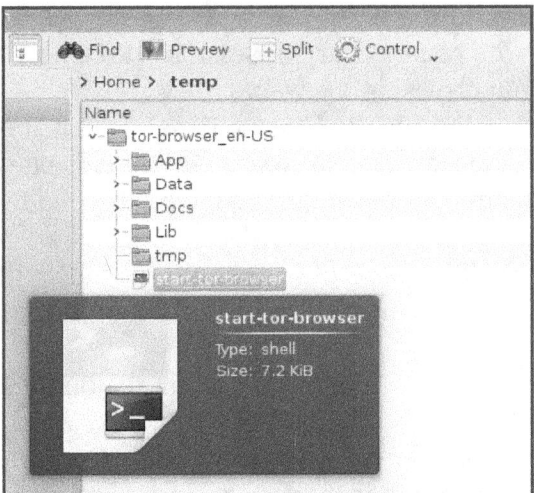

Double-click "Start Tor Browser" to start Tor. As Tor starts up, you'll see an onion icon in your system tray. The onion icon will start out yellow, indicating that you're connecting to the Tor network, then turn green once you're connected. You can right-click this icon to interact with Tor; it offers options for configuring Tor, as well as inspecting the state of the Tor network, restarting your session with a fresh IP address, and turning your PC into a Tor node, thereby making the Tor network a little better. Here's what the icon looks like before and after a right-click (I put a red circle around it in the left image):

 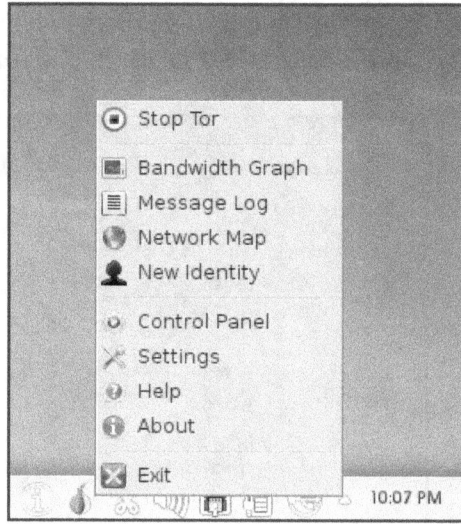

The items available to you do the following:

1. Stop Tor: Shuts down Tor on your PC and disconnects from the network.
2. Bandwidth Graph: Pops up a window showing you how much bandwidth you're using.
3. Message Log: Shows you any log entries Tor has saved (system events, errors, etc).
4. Network Map: Shows you the current set of Tor nodes you're interacting with, and how good their connections are.
5. New Identity: Lets you restart your Tor session with a new IP address, as if a whole new person had begun browsing the web.
6. Control Panel: Pops up the Vidalia Control Panel, which should usually start automatically when you start Tor. However, if you close it, you can re-open it here.
7. Settings: Allows you to configure Tor. You should probably read the help files first.
8. Help: A manual for the Tor system. You should read this.
9. About: A little information about your installation of Tor, including the version number.
10. Exit: Shut down Tor and exit Vidalia (the system the onion icon represents).

Along with the onion icon, you will see the "Vidalia Control Panel" on startup. This offers all the same options as the onion icon, with an additional option for turning your PC into a Tor node ("start relaying"). When Tor initially starts up, you'll see a progress bar indicating that Tor is connecting to its network. Once you're connected, the progress bar will turn into a green onion. You don't have to show this window on startup, but I like to. It looks like this:

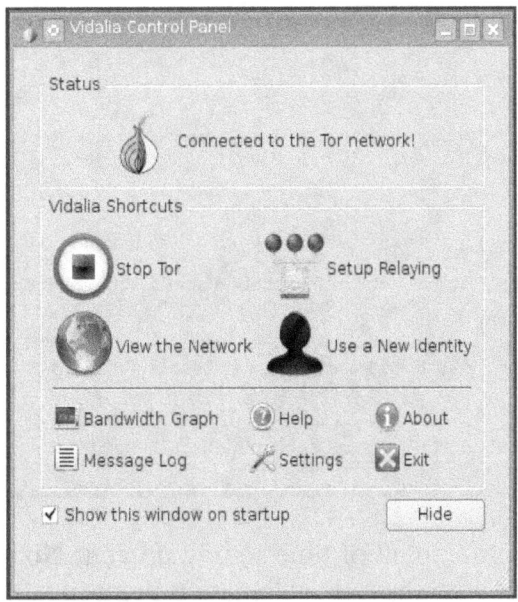

After about a minute, the Tor browser itself will start up. If you've used Mozilla Firefox in the past, the Tor browser will seem really familiar to you -- it seems to be a modified version of Firefox. It comes with NoScript and HTTPS Everywhere built in, and is preconfigured to be very secure. I don't recommend changing any of the settings, since they were set up to protect your privacy and anonymity.

The next image shows the Tor browser as it appears on startup. Note that by default, NoScript is blocking basically everything. This may sound restrictive, but blocking all active content makes it impossible for a web page to do much of anything to you. If something you want to connect to needs JavaScript to run, you can temporarily activate it by right-clicking the "S" icon in the white circle at the top left (I've drawn a circle around it in the image). It can be pretty eye-opening to see how many different companies are trying to run JavaScript when you browse an otherwise ordinary website. My suggestion is, only allow the website itself to run scripts, don't allow all the other third-party companies to run them. The less active content you allow to run in your browser, the more anonymous and secure you are.

Note: "Active content" basically means scripts, Java applets, Flash applications, or anything else that implements programming instructions when you visit a web page. In contrast, most web content is passive, a combination of text, images, and markup (like HTML and CSS). Passive content (mostly) can't do anything to you because it doesn't contain any programming; it exists to be viewed by you, and that's about it. One exception is something called a "web bug", a tiny little one pixel image, not even visible really, that only exists to record your IP address in the webserver's log files. Webmasters think they're very clever, and put these web bugs in to track you as you move from page to page within an advertising network, but when you run Tor, all they get is a bogus IP address. Lovely, isn't it?

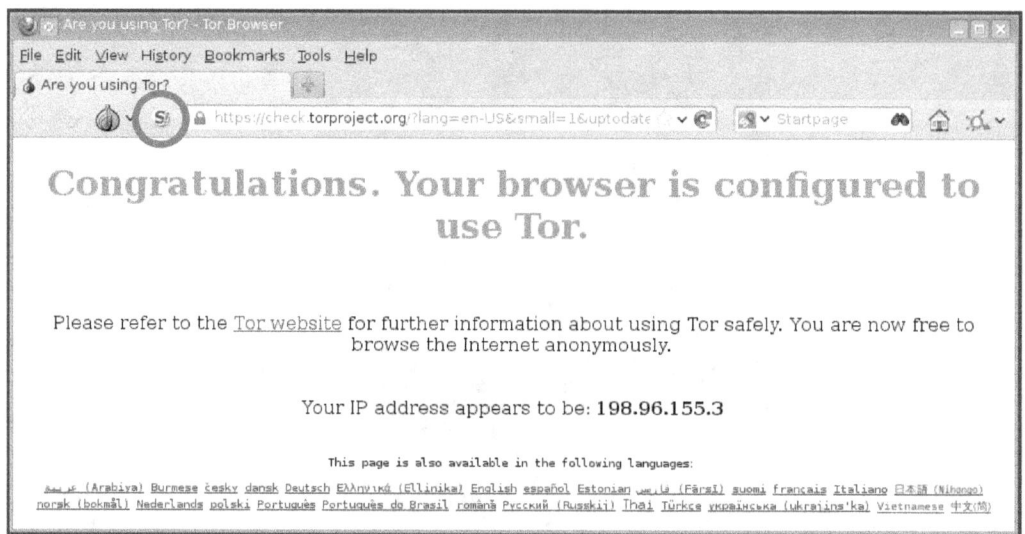

Let's spend a very short amount of time setting up your NoScript button (that's the white button on the upper left with the red exclamation point in it – again, I've drawn a circle around it in the above image). By default, NoScript in Tor is configured to deny all JavaScript everywhere. This is very safe, but some websites won't work at all with those settings, so what you need is a compromise position. What I like to do is set up NoScript so by default it denies everything, but you can temporarily allow specific domains to run scripts. This serves two purposes: First, you can see what sites are trying to run scripts in your browser, which is kind of interesting. Second, you can allow the website you're actually visiting to run scripts that make their site work, but deny the rest of the scripts (thereby killing off all the annoying ads and popups). Let's configure your NoScript and look at how to use it before we continue, it won't take long.

Configuring the Tor Browser's Script Protection

The Tor Browser is equipped with a tool called "NoScript" which protects you from the active elements found in modern web pages. It's able to prevent virtually all active content from running, and as a result is able to completely prevent a website from trying to find out more about you. It's important to keep this tool running, but there's a small problem with it. It's defaults are very strict, and if you leave them as-is you won't find much of the web usable.

What we're going to do in this section is configure NoScript with some very sensible settings that will completely protect you, but also allow you to permit some active content on web pages you personally trust. You'll have to keep in mind that you should only enable active content with great caution. If you're concerned that a site might try to track or identify you, it's probably a better idea not to enable any active content at all. You've got to weigh each situation on its merits, and make a decision.

These are the settings I use in all my browsers, so the recommendations I'm making here are the ones that have worked for me in practice for several years. I'll try to explain the reasoning behind each one as we go. Let's start with the actual NoScript button as it appears when you first run the Tor Browser; as I described earlier, it's essentially a round white button with a blue "S" and a red exclamation point. In this screenshot, you can see it between the Tor onion and the URL bar:

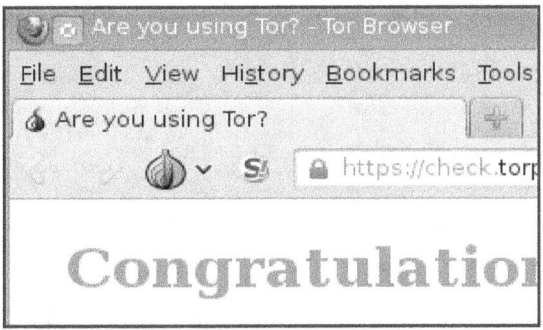

In order to configure NoScript, you'll have to right-click the S! button, then click "Options". The following configuration window will appear, within which you will be able to set all of the options available in NoScript. Please look at each screenshot I've provided you, and configure the matching section in your copy of NoScript the same way (but feel free to make sensible changes if you so desire).

When the Options window first appears, you'll start on the "Advanced" tab. There's nothing to do here, since these settings are fine. So click on the "General" tab (the first one) instead. You should see something like the screenshot on the next page. As you go through the next several pages, copy my settings; *I'll show you each new tab with a screenshot, and explain the settings under the screenshot.*

Start with the "General" tab, as seen below:

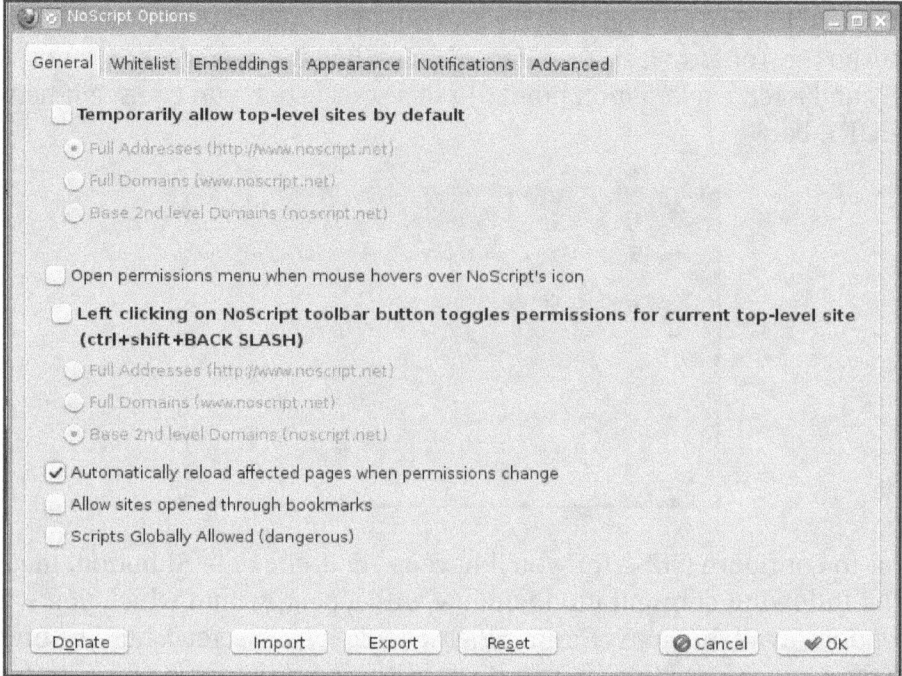

I unchecked "Temporarily allow top-level sites by default" because you never want to automatically enable anything on a web page within Tor. You want to manually decide what you're going to allow, remember, we're trying to protect our anonymity by using the Tor Browser. Don't throw away all protection!

I unchecked "Open permissions menu when mouse hovers over NoScript's icon" because it was annoying me to have the menu pop up every time the mouse pointer passed over the button. This was a usability issue for me. With this unchecked, you right-click the icon to see the menu but it stays out of the way otherwise. I find this more user-friendly.

I unchecked the "left click to toggle permissions" because I prefer to actually look at the permissions I'm granting, so I know what's going on. Toggling is convenient, but you don't get to see the list of sites trying to run content, so I disabled it.

I checked the "Automatically reload affected pages when permissions change" feature because it's very useful. If you don't reload the page, the change in permissions won't take effect. This is a time saver, because it prevents you from having to manually reload.

I unchecked the remaining two features, "Allow pages opened through bookmarks" and "Allow scripts globally" because I considered them dangerous. Again, you want to be able to see the permissions you're granting for yourself. You're using Tor, so be mindful about security.

There's nothing to do on the "Whitelist" tab, so skip ahead to the third tab, "Embeddings", which you can see in the next image.

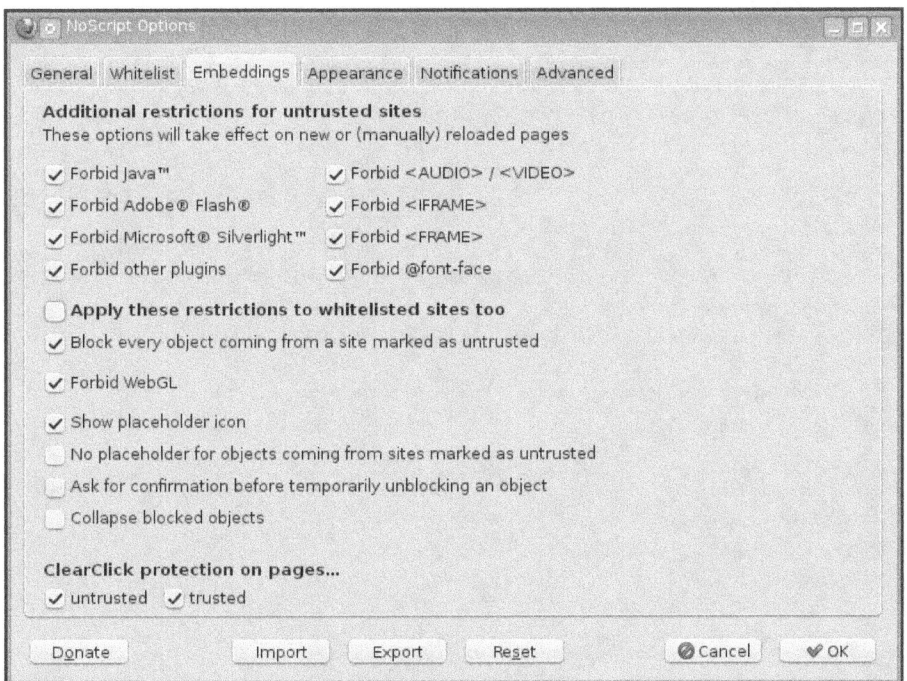

This is the tab where you can define what NoScript will protect you from. Check all the additional restrictions, and uncheck "Apply these restrictions to whitelisted sites too" (the point of a whitelisted site is that you've decided to allow active content to run; if you've whitelisted YouTube or LiveLeak, but you're still applying the restriction against Flash, you won't see any video).

I've also checked "block every object coming from a site marked as untrusted" because that's a sensible thing to do. I've forbidden WebGL, which is used for online video games and simulations, and could be used to attack a browser. I've checked "Show placeholder icon" because it's nice to be able to see the blocked items on a website. I've unchecked "No placeholder for objects coming from sites marked as untrusted" because I prefer to see the placeholders. I unchecked "Ask for confirmation before temporarily unblocking an object" because the confirmation windows are an annoyance. I unchecked "Collapse blocked objects" because that messes up page layout. I enabled ClearClick protection for both untrusted and trusted pages, because it's safer to keep that enabled.

Now, click on the "Appearance" tab, where we'll set up what NoScript will present to us while we're browsing the web. You can see it on the next page; this is where we'll eliminate clutter in the NoScript user interface.

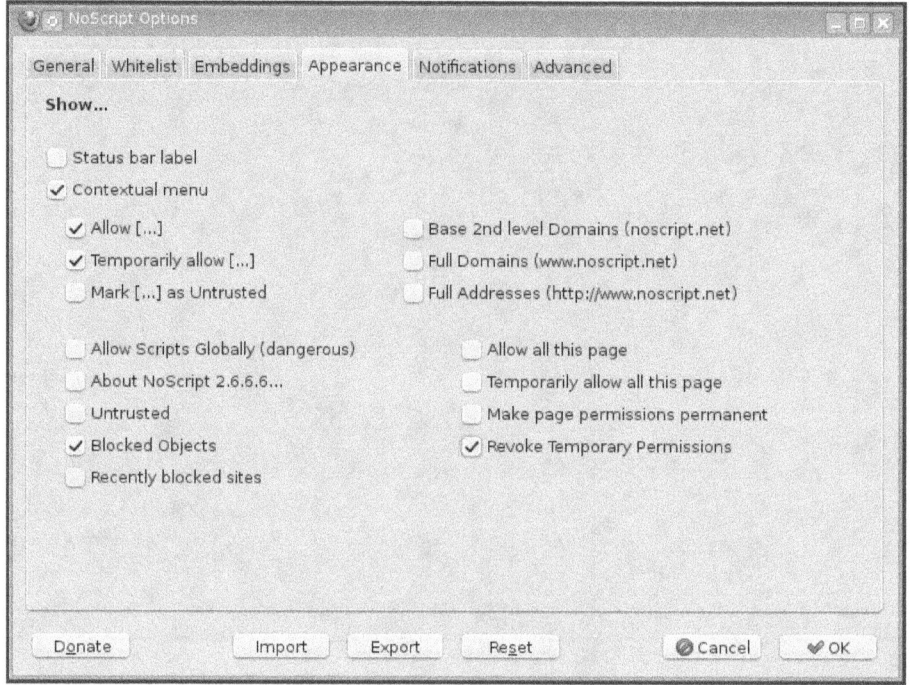

Here, I disabled the "Status bar label" because I didn't feel I needed it. I enabled the contextual menu, because that's how you enable or disable specific content, and I find it enormously useful. I enabled "Enable..." and "Temporarily Enable" but disabled "Mark as Untrusted" and the three domain-related settings. I think these two features are the most important: they allow us to permanently enable a domain to serve us active content, and to temporarily enable a domain to. These work only one domain at a time, and force us to think about what we're enabling.

I disabled "Allow scripts globally" because you should never, ever do that. I disabled "About NoScript" because it isn't related to the task at hand and I didn't want to clutter the interface. I disabled "Untrusted" because I think it's easier to just think of things as "Enabled" or "Disabled". I disabled "allow all this page" because, again, I don't want to make sweeping decisions without looking at the individual permissions I'm granting. I disabled "temporarily allow all this page" because although I use this in non-Tor browsers, if I'm using Tor and trying to be anonymous, I want to be more careful and look at all the permissions I'm granting. I disabled "Make page permissions permanent" because if I'm temporarily allowing permissions, I want them to stay temporary.

I enabled "Blocked objects" because it's nice to be able to see what NoScript is blocking. I enabled "Revoke temporary permissions" because it's nice to be able to change my mind about a permission I've granted. Finally, I disabled "Recently blocked sites" because it didn't interest me individually and I didn't want to clutter the interface.

In the next image, you can see the "Notifications" tab, which is the last one we'll be adjusting.

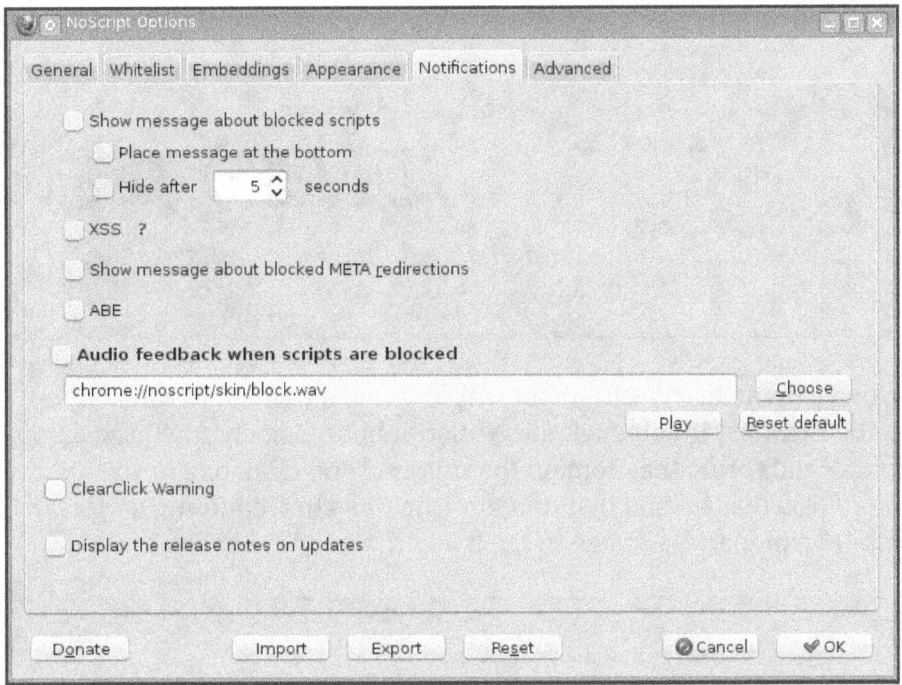

I generally disable all the notifications because I find them annoying. I start each web page with all active content disabled, and I only enable things I specifically want to enable, so I don't need to see notifications anyway. I know perfectly well that active content has been disabled. Why put up with distractions?

At this point we're done, so you should click "OK" to finalize your settings.

Next we'll look at how to interact with actual web pages and enable or disable content. Right or left clicking on the NoScript button will bring up the context menu, as shown in the next screenshot. We'll look at YouTube as an example first, because it's relatively clean, and doesn't have too much active content to consider. There are only two domains to worry about here, youtube.com and ytimg.com. As you can see, we can temporarily enable them, or permanently enable them. Every time you make a change, the website is reloaded and you can see the effect of the change.

Here's an image showing the NoScript options for YouTube (note that I've used a "mosaic" filter to conceal the video image in the background as a courtesy):

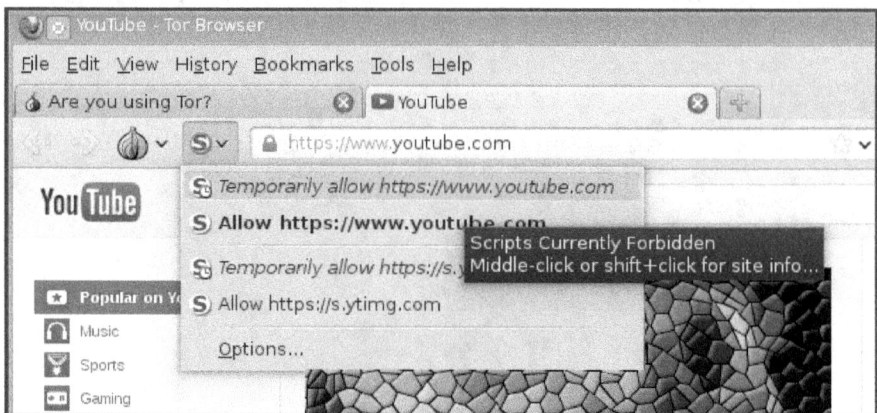

Once you've permanently or temporarily enabled a domain to run active content in the Tor Browser, if you click the NoScript button again you'll see an option to change your mind, and forbid that domain the right. If you click one of the "Forbid" items, the website will be reloaded again and that domain won't be allowed to run scripts in Tor Browser anymore. Again, I've hidden the image in the background with a mosaic.

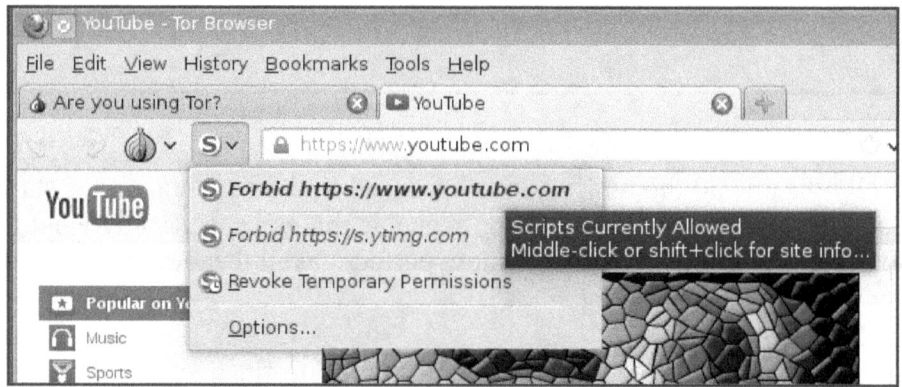

So far, this is all pretty simple, isn't it? Whenever you go to a website, if the website seems to require JavaScript (as some forums do) or something you want to access isn't working, just click the NoScript button and see what domains are trying to run active content. If you trust the domain enough to let them run content in your browser (this is ultimately up to you), you can either temporarily or permanently grant them permission to do so. If you change your mind, you can revoke it. The settings we configured earlier made this process as simple and direct as possible.

At this point, you should be relatively comfortable with the basic idea of NoScript, and you should be able to turn on what you need to make the sites you want to browse useful to you. This really is just about all there is to it. It's not rocket science.

Before I go, I'd like to point out that like YouTube, most websites are fairly well behaved and only host active content from a few domains. It's usually pretty easy to see what you should enable and what you should leave disabled (advertising networks, in particular, because they're all about tracking and identifying you). However, there are some websites out there that host active content from up to 30 or 40 different domains. Usually these are consumer-oriented sites, like personal technology magazines. The majority of the active content on these pages relates to two related things: advertising content, like popup windows, and advertising companies' tracking tools designed to identify you. Both present a significant threat to your anonymity.

My advice about pages like this is, enable as little as possible to make the content you're after available to you. Start with the web page's domain itself, then try to figure out the source of the content you actually want to look at (for example, if a site is linking to a JavaScript-based forum library, and their forum won't work without it, you'll want to find and enable the domain providing the forum library in NoScript, but nothing else). To figure out whether a domain is an advertiser you want to avoid, just use Wikipedia or Google in another tab, and check them out.

It's like a game, if you think about it. You want to enable as little as possible but still use the website. It can be a lot of fun, so enjoy it, and remember, use caution.

A Note on the Use of Proxies

One feature Tor offers is the ability to connect to the Tor network via a "proxy" or "bridge", i.e. a server configured to relay Internet traffic. The idea is, you're not connected to Tor, you're connected to the proxy, and the proxy forwards your connection onward to Tor. This prevents your ISP from knowing that you're connecting via Tor, and prevents anyone from simply blocking Tor traffic entirely. It sounds great, right?

This is going to make me sound paranoid, but I'm going to advise against the use of proxies and suggest that you always connect directly to Tor. When you connect to Tor, you're connecting to a network which is randomized. You're not going to be connecting to the same entry node all the time, and you'll get a different exit node every time you click the black silhouette to change your "identity". This makes it hard to predict how you're connecting to the network, and hard to set up a trap to try and identify you.

However, a proxy is a fixed, known point. You're connecting to a single server which is not a part of Tor, and using that to connect yourself to Tor. In other words, you're going through a middleman, and you're granting it an enormous amount of trust.

Imagine for a moment that you're the NSA, or a corporation, or some nosy foreign government. You have a nearly infinite amount of money available to you, and you want to be able to capture the data being passed by people who are connecting to Tor. You can't reliably do so within Tor, because the nodes you connect through tend to change, but you can buy some proxies and configure them to perform a "man in the middle" attack. How this works is, you set up the proxy to trick a user's browser into thinking it's connecting over SSL when it's really not, and you trick the server on the other side into thinking its SSL connection goes all the way through to the user when it doesn't. Then, you log all the now-unencrypted traffic that passes through your proxy. This is already a pretty well known attack against SSL, and you can download proxy software to accomplish it -- you don't even have to develop anything new. You can Google for "Man in the middle proxy" to see a few.

While we're on the topic, a nefarious government agency could also attack your anonymity in Tor by configuring the proxy to "tag" your connection, and watch the other side of Tor for the tag to come back out again. Then, they can use the tag to correlate the two endpoints of your Tor connection and presto! You're hosed. Note that they could theoretically also do that by messing with a Tor entry node, but since you don't necessarily know which one a person's going to be using, *they can't do it reliably* -- at least not as reliably as they can with a fixed proxy. There's some talk on the web about a government being able to set up enough Tor nodes to get lucky and own both your entry and exit nodes, but that would be incredibly unreliable. When I use Tor and I check the network status, I see nodes from all over the world, mostly in Europe, so I'm not terribly worried about that possibility. I think the most reliable way for a government agency or corporation to capture traffic would be to set up a hacked proxy server and trick people into using it to connect to Tor.

The bottom line is, I don't feel comfortable configuring Tor to use a proxy service. In my opinion, you can never know for sure whether they're being run by a government agency or corporation and logging your traffic. *It's better to connect directly to a randomly chosen Tor entry point, even if that means your ISP is aware you're doing it. For an extra layer of anonymity, you can go through a Wi-Fi hotspot somewhere away from home, preferably a medium-to-large city where you won't be remembered. But! There's a caveat there!*

On the Use of Wi-Fi Hotspots

There's a similar issue with the use of Wi-Fi hotspots. Anything you send over Wi-Fi can potentially be interfered with, captured, or otherwise messed with. There have been proof of concept experiments in which hackers have configured their laptops to act as SSL-intercepting proxies (like we just talked about), and they've tricked people using Wi-Fi hotspots into connecting through their proxy instead of going directly to the hotspot. This way, they've been able to capture people's passwords and other Internet traffic. Anyone at the cafe offering the hotspot could be doing this, even the employees. Obviously, this is a concern for Tor and anonymity as well. *Remember to be particularly careful about using publicly available Wi-Fi; make SURE you're connecting to the right hotspot, make SURE you're connecting via SSL, and make SURE the SSL certificates are genuine.* Work with your anonymous email, post to your anonyous forums, and if you feel nervous about anything that happened at the hotspot, log back in via Tor and change your passwords when you get back to your home or hotel. It may sound paranoid, but it's better to be safe than sorry, and it's generally a good idea to trust your instincts. If something at the Wi-Fi hotspot made you nervous, maybe there's a reason -- maybe your subconscious picked up on some cues your conscious mind missed. Trust your gut.

The Other Side of the Coin: Setting Up Anonymous Webmail

Using Tor is important, but it's not sufficient. You also need to have at least a few anonymous webmail accounts. *These are critically important because they allow you to sign up for websites and forums you want to participate in without giving away your identity.* Tor is one half of a coin; anonymous email is the other half. If you use them together, you can enjoy fairly strong anonymity on the Internet.

You should think of email (and email validation, which websites use to identify people) as a trap, one which can completely obliterate your attempts to stay anonymous. To see why this is the case, let's perform a little thought experiment.

Let's say you've decided to start discussing a political topic on a certain website forum. You've already read part of this book, so you fire up Tor, you browse to the website, and you try to join the conversation. Unfortunately, you learn that you have to sign up for a forum account if you want to participate. So you begin the sign up process, and you give them a pen name because you want to remain anonymous. Then they ask you for your email, so they can "validate" you, and "activate" your account. You know that you can't sign up unless you give them a working email address. You've seen this before, they're going to send you an email and you're going to have to click something in it. So you give them an email address, probably a webmail account you've been using for a while, and they send you their validation email.

Still in Tor, you check your webmail account. When the email arrives, it's got graphical elements and it's got a link for you to click to "validate" or "activate" your account. You click the link, it opens another Tor browser window, and your account is created. You log into the website, you go into your account details, and you delete the email address. Are you now anonymous? Can you safely say whatever you want, without having to worry about being persecuted? After all, you're using Tor, right?

No, you are not anonymous. First of all, your email address is still stored somewhere in their system, along with the IP address you had when you clicked the "validate" link and a timestamp. It's stored as metadata, giving them some record of who created the account in case the government ever asks for it. It's lucky you were using Tor at the time, and the IP address wasn't able to be linked to you, but *they have the email address* and *that's a problem. If you've ever accessed that webmail account without using Tor, your real IP address will be available in the webmail provider's logs and this will directly identify you.* All a lawyer or investigator would have to do is work backwards through their logs until he finds a non-Tor IP address. That and its timestamp can be taken to your ISP, which can look up who had that IP address at that exact time (depending on how good they are at logging this sort of thing). Worse, what they can do is match up the Tor IP addresses in your email provider's logs with the Tor IP addresses they find in any other forums they might be interested in, and "connect the dots". In other words, each IP address in the email provider's logs would confirm that you were online using Tor with that exit node at that time. They could match that with your other online activity and link it all together by Tor exit node. It's circumstantial, but that's more than enough to let them start picking on you.

Here's something else that you might find interesting. When you view a graphical email, like the ones websites use for validation, the content is generally "active" content and is being served by the website itself. *This means that when you look at the email, you're downloading all the images and content in it, and the website providing them logs your IP address for each download. If you ever look at that email without using Tor, your real IP address will be logged and you'll be revealed.* As long as such an email sits in your webmail account, it's like a mousetrap waiting for you to look at it. Forget to use Tor even once, and you're no longer anonymous.

Hopefully you can see that email validation is the second biggest threat to your online anonymity (after having your real IP address logged, which Tor takes care of if you're careful). If you don't use an anonymous email account to set up anonymous forum accounts, and you don't carefully use Tor whenever you're accessing *any* of these anonymous accounts, *you're completely hosed. All it takes is one slip up, one log entry to positively identify you and they can tie everything else you do together.*

Now let's do another thought experiment, and see if we can use Tor along with anonymous email accounts to successfully remain anonymous.

First, let's assume that we've spent some time creating some webmail accounts while using Tor. We could bookmark their login pages only in the Tor Browser so we won't accidentally access them outside of Tor. We could make sure we don't put any personally identifying information in these webmail accounts. Also, we'd use a pseudonym or nickname, something that can't be tied to us. These accounts would be reserved only for doing anonymous things, like setting up anonymous forum accounts or anonymously reporting a problem to the press. We wouldn't use them for anything related to our daily lives.

Next, while still using Tor, we'd register for the forum we wanted to participate in. We'd supply one of our brand-new anonymous email addresses when they demanded validation, and we'd open a new tab in the Tor Browser to log into our anonymous webmail account and click the validation link. This way, we'd still be in Tor when the validation link opened a new tab and logged us into the forum.

As we interacted with the forum and expressed our opinions on various and sundry topics, perhaps convincing other people that our positions are correct, we would *always* be running Tor and we would *never* reveal anything too specific about ourselves. We'd stay "on topic" and only talk about the issues we wanted to discuss.

Assuming that we've done all that and been careful about it, what would happen if someone powerful decided they didn't like what we had to say and tried to shut us down? Let's assume they'll send their lawyers after the website like they did in the previous experiment.

The first thing the lawyers will do is subpoena the forum site, which will hand over all the web server logs, copies of our forum conversations, and our account metadata. None of this will identify us; every IP address they'll find will turn out to be a Tor exit node. None of our comments will identify us either. Frustrated, they'll turn to the email address we used to sign up for the site. Sending a subpoena to the email provider, they'll get their IP logs as well as all our email and our account metadata. All of these IP addresses will turn out to be Tor exit nodes, too, and there'll be no personally identifying information anywhere in our account. Our emails will only contain talk about the forum, and will mention nothing the investigators don't already know.

This time, they'll have hit a brick wall. They literally can't persecute us for expressing our opinions; they can't even figure out who we are. They will have spent thousands of dollars and a lot of time and energy to secure nothing but a big old digital goose egg.

Anonymous email: it's such a simple thing, but very important. Without it, you can't be anonymous on the web because many websites use some form of email validation. But we have Tor, and with Tor and a little cleverness, we can get all the anonymous email accounts we will ever need.

Using Tor to Find Suitable Providers and
Set Up Anonymous Email Accounts

First, let me explain what I mean by "suitable providers". I consider a suitable provider of anonymous webmail to be one who:

1) Doesn't require any form of email validation to set up an account.

2) Doesn't require payment of any kind for setting up an account, because it is virtually impossible to pay anyone for anything without revealing your identity and making the whole thing completely pointless. Most suitable providers are supported by advertising.

3) Doesn't block Tor (some companies do). Technically we could use proxies, but why bother? Just find someone who doesn't block Tor.

With that understood, we can fire up Tor and search the web for providers. You have two options here; you can just go straight to Google.com, which I generally like to do, or you can use the search tool available within Tor, in the upper right hand corner. Let's use Google. Note that sometimes, Google blocks some of the Tor exit nodes. I assume this means someone was messing with them and they had to lock him out. They never block all of Tor, so if your current exit node is blocked just click the black human silhouette in the Tor control panel to change exit nodes (and get a new IP address).

My search term will be the very simple "free anonymous webmail". I used "webmail" instead of "email" because I want to access the email only from within Tor, and that requires it be provided via a website. The term "email" is too broad, including POP and IMAP services, which we won't be bothering with. This search produces a lot of results; go ahead and try it yourself (remember to use Tor). Here's what I got:

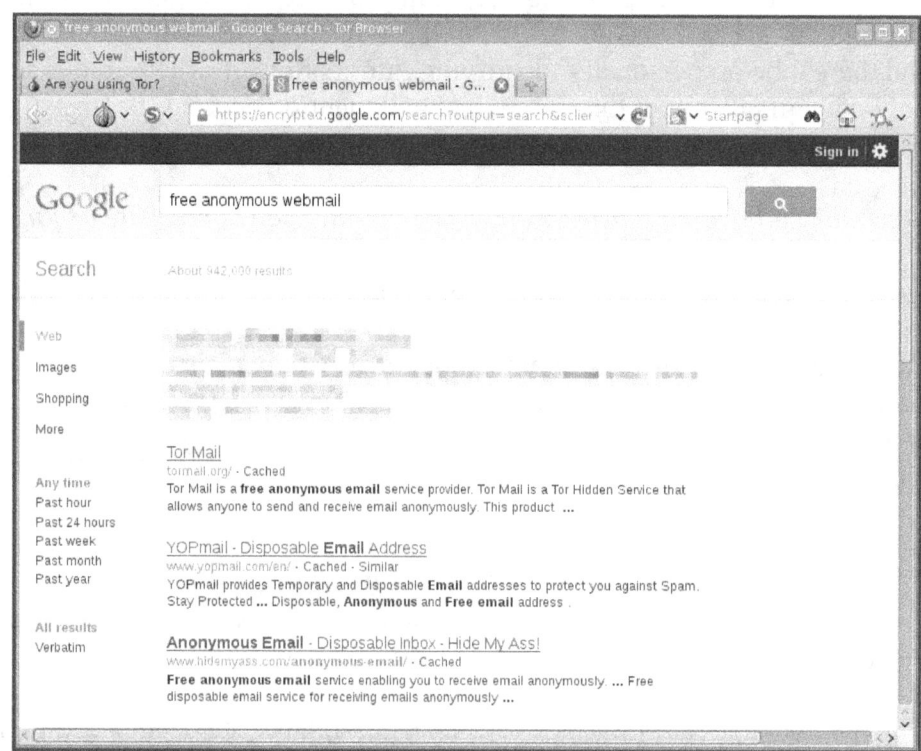

Right off the bat, we've got some good providers here. Actually, there are almost a million search results. I decided to noodle around a little and see whether any of these would suit my purposes. Here are a few recommendations from the first few pages of results, in case you want to fire up Tor and set up some accounts (I've blurred out the first link that came up, because it really didn't suit our purposes here):

1) Tor Mail (https://tormail.org): Tor Mail is an absolutely amazing idea. Seriously, you should go to their website just to read it, it's incredibly interesting. First of all, tormail.org isn't even their mail server; it's just their way of saying "Hello" and announcing their current site address, which they could change if they like. The mail server is on a hidden Tor service which is only accessible within the Tor network. It's impossible to track down its location, and there's no way to identify whoever's running it. They have anonymity-friendly policies; opening an account is easy and quick, they don't require any personal information, and they don't require any email validation. Because the site's encrypted with SSL, your email content won't get automatically captured by the government in transit. Also, since you can't even

access their mail server outside Tor, there's no way for them to know any more about you than you know about them. Interesting!

2) Hide My Ass! (https://www.hidemyass.com): Here's another great service (which I've just signed up for). The site's got a great logo, too -- a donkey dressed up like a film noir private detective. They don't require any personal information and there's no activation process; although they *allow* you to supply an alternate email address, they don't *require* one (very classy). Their site works fine within Tor, it's encrypted with SSL so you don't have to worry about eavesdropping, and they offer a *really* interesting feature: you can choose an expiration date for your account, so it gets completely deleted after one of several time periods they offer (the shortest is 24 hours, and the longest is one year). They seem to offer an outstanding service; I really like these guys.

3) Yahoo.com (https://mail.yahoo.com): OK, this seems really counter-intuitive since they're such a big U.S. company, but Yahoo is completely Tor friendly. You can access Yahoo mail from within Tor with no problem whatsoever, including over SSL, so that's nice. Setting up an anonymous email account is easy, too, you just have to pick a name which isn't already in use (they'll warn you if someone already has the user ID you asked for). Pick something weird and random, and you're unlikely to conflict with any existing users. They ask for your birthdate and zipcode, presumably for marketing purposes, but you can put anything in. Because you'll be accessing the site from Tor (remember?) Yahoo won't know what country you're in -- I showed up as being in Sweden, so at first they put me on their German language site for some reason. But you can change "de" to "us" in the URL and reload to go back to their main U.S. site. To make it through their registration form, you have to temporarily allow JavaScript, but it looks like they only use it for error-checking and telling you how strong your password is; they aren't doing anything sneaky from what I could see. I had a little trouble with their captcha; man, they have a tough captcha. It's very pretty, like white paper text floating in water, but it's really hard to get all the letters right. It took me about ten tries (I guess I'm getting old -- bad eyesight!). Still, in the end I had a completely anonymous email account, at Yahoo, one of the more stable, long-lived companies on the web. As a test, I sent myself an email and checked the headers: the originating IP address was my Tor exit node address, somewhere in Denmark, I think. Result.

4) I'd like to take a moment and mention mail.com, a very good email provider whose sign-up website I couldn't access via Tor. It's a real shame, because they're an excellent email provider and they don't require validation. They even let you choose from dozens of possible domains, like "technologist.com" or "programmer.net". Being unable to sign up within Tor is remarkably frustrating, particularly because normal account logins work just fine within Tor. However, all is not lost... All you have to do is find a coffee shop that offers public Wi-Fi access in a town at least a half hour away (farther is better), so your IP address during the session can't be automatically tied to you. *Dress conservatively, pay cash, be as boring and unremarkable as you can, and don't give any personal details to the coffee shop staff.* While there, use the mail.com signup page to create a few accounts, giving them nothing that would identify you. Once the accounts are created, you should be able to do everything else via Tor. Then, don't go back to that coffee shop for a long while (give them time to completely forget

about you). Also, when you log in via Tor, make sure you change the password in case anyone at the cafe managed to log your traffic via some kind of intercepting proxy.

5) YOPMail (http://www.yopmail.com/en/): Here's another amazing service. YOPMail stands for "Your Own Protection Mail", and the idea behind their service is that you can create a completely anonymous, temporary email address specifically to sign up for a website. Just make something up, like "JoeSchmoe12345@yopmail.com" when you sign up for the website. As soon as the email arrives at their server, they create a temporary email account for you to receive that email. Then, you can go to YOPMail's website, log in automatically (there's no site registration and no password necessary), view your email, click the activation link, and forget all about it. YOPMail emails are deleted automatically after eight days. This seems to be a very good way of maintaining forum anonymity.

6) Mailnesia (http://mailnesia.com/): This service is similar to YOPMail, with one added wrinkle: when they receive an email from a forum site you've signed up with, they automatically click the confirmation link for you. Other than that, it seems like a very similar service, allowing you to join online forums without revealing yourself to them. Again, this seems like a good way of maintaining forum anonymity.

Some Pointers For Setting Up Your Accounts:

When you're signing up for an anonymous email account, r*emember not to use your real name.* Use a handle, something that can't be tied directly to you. Don't pick something that someone could guess is yours. Don't use something that relates to your private life. Pick something different, and random. For example, when I set up an anonymous email account, I'll use something like Jack Flash, or John Smith, something that doesn't relate to me in any way. There's nothing wrong with this, and it's certainly not illegal to role-play online, so have fun with it. Come up with something interesting, or funny.

While we're on the subject of anonymous email, I'd like to mention that you shouldn't limit yourself to only one anonymous account. In fact, you should create several of them, at least one for each website you use which might cause you trouble.

Let's say you want to speak your mind on four separate website forums. Let's make them really political; how about gun rights, abortion rights, gay marriage, and a union squabble. It's fairly safe to assume that in at least one of those forums, you're going to piss off somebody who is able to try and track you down. It could be an arrogant politician, a police officer who doesn't like what you're saying, or even just some random crazy person with too much time on his hands. So, each of these forums you participate in increases your chances of being placed under someone's scrutiny.

If you use the same anonymous email account to participate in all four forums, then it becomes a central point of failure for your anonymity. A problem in one forum can lead to someone using their lawyer to get a subpoena for the email provider. Then, they can read your email and figure out that you're participating in all four forums. From there, they can try to put together a picture of who you really are. The more of your posts they can analyze, the more likely it is they'll learn something about you. Did you accidentally reveal something in a forum comment? Will they find it? You want to limit this sort of scrutiny as much as possible.

All you have to do is create a separate anonymous email address for each of the four forums. This way, if anyone takes an interest in your activity on any one forum, they can't link that email address to the other forums and tie them all together. They'll only be able to scrutinize the one email address, and since you only use it for that specific forum, and you only access it via Tor, it'll be a dead end. Not only will there be nothing in any email that doesn't relate to the forum itself, the mail server's logs will only contain useless, anonymized Tor IP addresses.

Another nice feature of this approach is that you can dump any account that makes you nervous. If you decide things are getting too weird in one of the forums, you can close the related accounts and wash your hands of the whole thing without affecting your other forum accounts. By separating out the different email addresses and forum accounts, you've given yourself the equivalent of an ejection seat.

I should point out that we're not only worried about the government or arrogant politicians, here. You might express an opinion in one of your forums that pisses off some random psychopath. The Internet has a whole lot of crazy, crazy people in it. Some of them get ridiculously angry over the dumbest stuff. You don't want them being able to figure out who you are. You don't want them being able to buy your address from one of the multitude of "people search" sites out there, so they can turn up at your house and knock on your door. Posting anonymously is like magic the way it lets you avoid encounters with the crazy basement dwellers of the Internet.

Signing up for Websites and Forums Anonymously

So, now you have a few anonymous email accounts, and you're getting used to using Tor. Your next step is to sign up for any website forums in which you'd like to safely and anonymously express your opinion. Forum chat isn't just blather, regardless of what anyone might think. Blogs, blog comments, and forum comments can be very influential in our online society. An eloquently written post, sharing valid information, can change people's minds. You can convince people of your point of view, and they will go on to convince other people, and so on. If enough people agree with a position, it might even get traction with politicians and result in change. So it's a very positive thing to argue a position online. You just don't want to get persecuted because the government, or your boss, or your neighbors, disagree with something you said.

So, again, fire up Tor. Using the Tor browser, log in to one of your anonymous email accounts. Then, open another tab in the Tor browser, and visit the website or forum you want to participate in. Sign up for an account just like you did with the anonymous email account, again providing a handle and info that can't be tied back to you. Provide your anonymous email account for validation. They'll send a validation email, so go back to your email account tab, open their email, and click the link to validate it. When you're done, you have both an anonymous email account and an anonymous forum account.

Now, remember not to say anything via anonymous email or the anonymous forum account that would let anyone guess who you actually are. The whole idea here is to be anonymous. Don't talk about recognizable events in your real life, or your town, or your car, or house, or anything else that anyone could use to identify you. Stick to the issues you want to talk about. Remember not to lose your temper, or threaten anyone, or otherwise do anything that would give the government or the police an excuse to chase you. Keep it polite, and keep it reasonable.

Here's a tip about passwords... If you keep a password book around your house, or you write them down anywhere, sooner or later somebody's going to see them and your anonymity will be torn to bits. So don't keep track of your anonymous accounts anywhere but in your head. Pick easy to remember handles, and use a common pass phrase for all your related anonymous accounts. Choose a line of poetry you like, for example, something easy to remember. Now nobody can figure out who you're posting as by snooping around your house, and your family can't accidentally stumble on it and "out" you by accident.

Finally, you might want to think about retiring your accounts after some period of time. If some crazy forum person has decided that your Billy Bob persona is their mortal enemy, stop using that account and create another one, so you can post in peace and quiet. Sooner or later, the crazy person will settle down and forget all about Billy Bob, fixating on someone else. You can decide how you want to interact with the forum, you don't have to play by the crazy person's rules. Be a ghost. Be impossible to nail down. There's nothing wrong with using your anonymity to your advantage.

Using Tor and Anonymity to Learn Things

There's one last thing Tor and anonymity are good for. They're great for learning things that society at large considers dodgy, or suspect. I'm going to give you what I consider to be the classic example: security research, aka computer hacking.

If you're not a technology professional, you might not know that there are legitimate reasons why someone would want to learn about hacking. Take me for instance. I'm a Java programmer by trade, and I've also been an Oracle database administrator and system administrator. When you're performing these roles, one of your duties is maintaining the security of your systems. The only way to do that is by learning about hacking, so you know what people are going to try and you know how to lock them out.

But learning about it is really tricky, because society has stigmatized hacking, and any interest in it or research about it is looked upon as inherently suspicious by our government and our ISPs. So let's say you're running a Windows 2005 server, and you want to see how people might try to hack into it. You want to know what you should worry about, so you try to do a web search on that. You're going to throw up a lot of red flags, and you can be sure that somebody's going to be paying attention to you for a while. Your ISP might take an interest; the NSA and FBI are likely to as well. They're all going to be wondering "what exactly is this guy up to?" They're not going to believe you're just curious, or that you're trying to study the subject. They're going to be suspicious.

I think this would be a nicer world if we could all just study whatever we wanted, satisfying our curiosity and reading whatever we liked, without anyone raising an eyebrow or flagging us for investigation. Sadly, we're stuck in a world where simply checking the wrong book out of the library can make the FBI take an interest in you. This is not an urban legend: The FBI is empowered by the Patriot Act and the "Attorney General's Guidelines on General Crimes, Racketeering and Terrorism" to demand library and bookstore records for groups of people, not just individuals. Here are two links from the American Library Association website.

This link leads to the ALA's Patriot Act FAQ:
http://www.ala.org/offices/oif/ifissues/issuesrelatedlinks/usapatriotactfaq

This link leads to a general discussion of library-related privacy:
http://www.ala.org/offices/oif/iftoolkits/toolkitsprivacy/privacycommunication/messagestalkingpoints/keymessages

I have a rule: if a conservative authoritarian would give me the stink eye for reading something, I either read it right in the library without discussing it with the staff, I buy it for cash in a large, corporate bookstore where I won't be remembered, or I find it online while using Tor. That way, nobody knows I've looked at it and I can satisfy my curiosity without being hassled. What they don't know can't hurt you.

By using Tor properly, we can learn anything we want, read any books we want, and visit any websites we want, all without being investigated or persecuted or otherwise harassed. And that's a thing of beauty.

Some General Guidelines for Remaining Anonymous:

1) Mentally try and link the Tor Browser with all your anonymous accounts and activities, so you can't imagine accessing them without Tor. Store the bookmarks you use with these accounts *only* in the Tor browser, and don't use Firefox Sync. You don't want to accidentally open them in some other browser and leave your real IP address in a website's log file.

2) Remember that you have to use Tor from the "cradle to the grave". This means that you use Tor to create your anonymous accounts in the first place, you use Tor whenever you use the accounts, and you use Tor when it's time to close the accounts down for good. For the entire lifespan of your anonymous accounts, you *only* interact with them via Tor.

3) When you're using your anonymous accounts, don't do things that will give you away. For example, you can't ever spend money anonymously online, because the very act of paying someone online involves identifying yourself. Similarly, don't talk about where you work, who your friends and family are, what kind of car or house you have, or what you look like. Every single thing you tell people is a piece of a puzzle that they'll eventually want to put together.

4) In your regular daily life, completely avoid politics and strife. Use your regular, non-anonymous accounts to keep in touch with your friends and family, browse the web, entertain yourself, and buy stuff. If the government wants to snoop on you, all they'll see is a very normal, super-boring guy. It's good to be that guy. It keeps everyone off your back. Celebrate your normalness.

5) But when you want to engage in a little activism, or try and do something to improve the world, or otherwise brush up against the political realm, remember: it's a whole lot safer when you use Tor and your anonymous accounts. If there's any chance you might get persecuted or attacked for something you want to say, say it anonymously! It's what Tor was made for.

6) Remember to be careful about proxies and Wi-Fi! If you use a Wi-Fi connection to post some things online and you suspect anything weird may have happened, as soon as you get home you should log back in via Tor and change the passwords on any sites you accessed.

7) Keep reminding yourself that there's nothing wrong with wanting to be anonymous online. Protecting yourself from all the crazy people on the Internet is smart, it's a good thing. Protecting yourself from a nosy, overreaching government is good too.

8) Like any tool, anonymity can be used for good or evil. Use it for good, and you have every right to feel good about it. Don't let anyone tell you any different.

Chapter 3:

***How to Protect Your Private Files and securely
Exchange Files Using the Gnu Privacy Guard
and Strong Encryption.***

A long time ago, back in the 1990's when I was still in college, an amazing guy named Phil Zimmerman created a system called Pretty Good Privacy. It was groundbreaking because it made strong encryption available to the general public for the first time in history. Previously only the government could use encryption, and most people didn't even know it existed. Of course, all Hell immediately broke loose. The government classified PGP as a "munition" for export purposes, there was a court case, the Internet was absolutely fascinated with the story, and eventually the government backed down and changed the rules enough that PGP could be distributed. It was fascinating for those of us who were following the story, and if you want to enjoy it yourself you can start at PGP's Wikipedia page and follow the links to read more about it.

PGP is still available, and still very good, but we're going to use its sibling the Gnu Privacy Guard, or GPG. It's available completely for free and does most of the same things PGP does. This chapter will take you through the steps of installing GPG and encrypting your personal files to protect them. Before we begin, there's one small point we have to address:

__Warning:__ The encryption methods I'm going to be telling you about are secure. This means, even the federal government will generally not be able to break them without your pass phrase (like a password, used for encryption and decryption). Your average busybody, like a nosy friend, boss, coworker, girlfriend or spouse, won't have even the slightest chance of breaking in. But this means that if you mess up and forget your pass phrase, you won't be getting back in either! __Nobody will, EVER__.

Whatever you choose for a pass phrase __must__ be something you can easily remember. I like to use a few lines from literature, something I can look up in case I forget it. Whatever you do, don't write it down; if you do that, some busybody will find your notes and decrypt your stuff. Memorize your pass phrase! And don't tell it to anybody.

The Gnu Privacy Guard on Fedora

The other editions of this book have whole sections on how to download GPG, how to set it up, and how to use third party tools with it. None of this nonsense is necessary on a Gnu/Linux system; Gnu/Linux is GnuPG's natural habitat. Installing it is as simple as opening up your software repository and selecting GnuPG for installation. All the tools you need come along with the install. It couldn't be easier.

Here's a screenshot of the Fedora software repository, after I did a search for "GnuPG". As you can see, its already installed by default. This makes things so much easier than they are on other operating systems... *On Fedora, everything just works.*

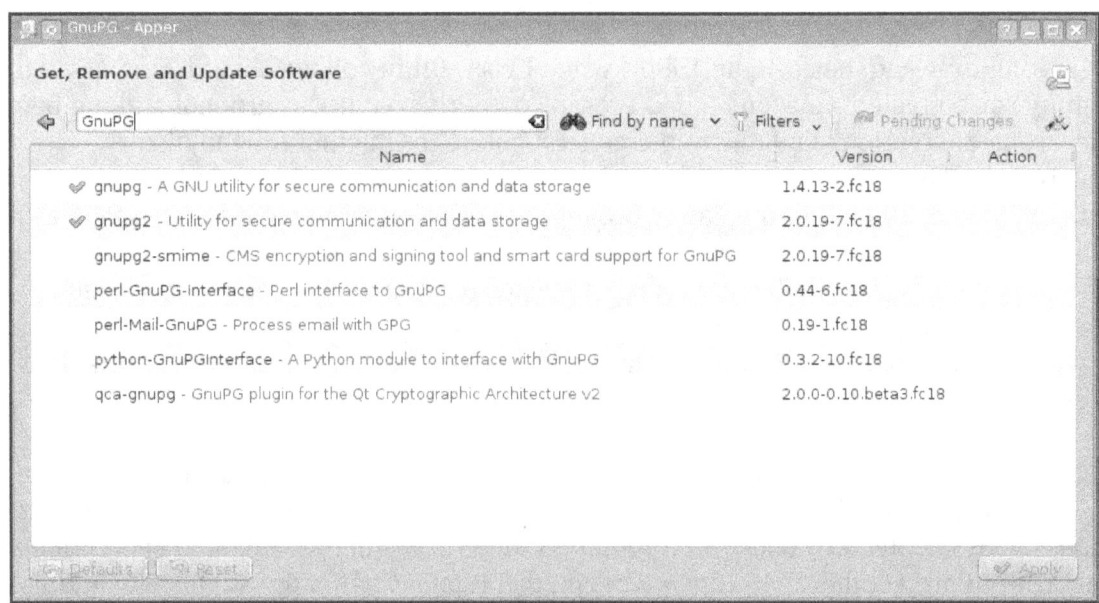

If you're like me, you're probably already chomping at the bit to start working with GnuPG, but before we get started, I'd like to go over some basic ideas about encryption. I'm not trying to pretend I'm some kind of expert, I'm just sharing what I know on the topic, and maybe a few very opinionated thoughts on the subject, before we dive in and start encrypting things. If you're already comfortable with encryption, you can safely skim over the next section and skip ahead to the good stuff. If not, this next part will make the rest of the chapter make a whole lot more sense.

An Introduction to Encryption: What it Is, What it's For

You don't have to be a mathematician, hacker, or government spy to use and understand encryption. After all, you don't have to be a master chef to scramble some eggs, you just need to get the basic idea and spend some time practicing. To further abuse my egg metaphor, this first section will tell you how to choose eggs, and explain the basic idea of how you scramble and cook them. Then, in the next section, we'll actually go into the kitchen, fire up the stove, beat some eggs, and get them in the frying pan. Don't worry, it's all much easier than you'd think.

Encryption is a way of scrambling the content of an email or a file so nobody can read it except you and possibly a person you want to send it to. The idea is to find a ridiculously difficult math problem like prime number factorization, a problem which computers can't solve in any reasonable amount of time. Then you use this problem to encode messages. For example, RSA encryption uses very large prime numbers multiplied by other very large prime numbers to create a very large integer which is then used to encrypt data. You can't decrypt the data without knowing the prime numbers, and if you wanted to use a computer to try and guess them, the computer would have to factor the resulting very large number, which would take an amazingly long time (on the order of millions of years if you use large enough numbers). I'm oversimplifying a little, here, but that's the basic idea.

There are two broad types of encryption that you'll want to use, each of which is useful for different things. First, there's **public key encryption**, which you'll want to use for sending encrypted messages to other people. Then, there's **symmetric key encryption**, which you'll want to use only for encrypting things you're keeping for yourself, like your personal files on your PC. Let's look at each of these.

Public key encryption, also called **asymetric encryption**, uses two "keys" to encrypt and decrypt files or messages. You give your public key to other people, and they use it to encrypt messages they want to send to you. When you receive an encrypted message, you use your secret key and a pass phrase to decrypt it. The public key is public knowledge -- you can even store it on a "key server" so other people can look you up, find your key, and encrypt things they want to send to you. The secret key is for your eyes only; you have to protect it, and prevent anyone else from getting their hands on it.

You can also digitally sign messages with your secret key, and when people receive the messages, they can test the signature with your public key to see if the messages really came from you. Similarly, they can sign their messages with their secret key, and you can test them with their public key. So public key encryption also gives you the ability to verify where messages came from.

Symmetric encryption uses the same key for encryption and decryption, so it doesn't require you to create any keys in advance. Instead, you just think up a pass phrase (preferably a long one you'll remember, like a line from an obscure poem you like, or the second sentence of the third chapter of a book you've read). This pass phrase is used by your encryption software to generate a key which is then used to encrypt your data. To decrypt the data, you'll have to supply the exact same pass phrase; everything has to be identical, including spaces and punctuation. Again, you want to pick a nice, long pass phrase, something that you'll remember but which can't be guessed easily. Throw a number in somewhere to make it a little harder for anyone to guess.

Whether you're using symmetric encryption or public key encryption, you'll have to choose which algorithm you want to use to do the actual encryption. Here's a list of the currently available algorithms, along with my opinion (based on what I've read) about whether they're secure.

For public key encryption, GnuPG supports the following algorithms:

RSA: Very secure (this one is my personal favorite). GPG will ask you how many bits you will want to use for your key (the more bits you use, the more secure your messages will be). The minimum is 1024 bits, the max is 4096, and the default is 2048. I generally use 4096. Supposedly, it's just about impossible to break the encryption on an RSA message which is encrypted using a 2048-bit key or higher. There's a good, but very technical, discussion on Stack Exchange about how safe RSA is. You can find it here, but it gets pretty deep:

http://security.stackexchange.com/questions/4518/how-to-estimate-the-time-needed-to-crack-rsa-encryption

The gist of the article is that nobody's actually cracked even a 1024-bit RSA key yet. Some of the best mathematicians in the world are currently working on a project that might do it, but as of 2013, they haven't done it yet. According to Wikipedia's RSA entry, as of 2010 mathematicians had only managed to break a 768-bit RSA key. Supposedly, it might be possible to crack a 1024-bit RSA key by 2020 or so. Use a higher bit length, and you're probably completely secure. Interestingly, according to the Stack Exchange article, when you visit a secure website like a banking site the encryption used in SSL is generally 1024-bit RSA.

ELG (El Gamal): El Gamal uses a different approach than RSA, and seems to be comparably secure. Like RSA, it's a public key encryption algorithm, and you can specify the bit length of your key. As with RSA, longer is better; 2048 bits is the default, 4096 is available. I think Europeans may have a bit of a preference for El Gamal, because when it came out it wasn't encumbered by any U.S. patents. I seem to remember there was a lot of discussion about this on Slashdot back then. At the time, RSA was still patented and required a license if you wanted to include it in your software, so free software programmers went with El Gamal instead. Luckily, the RSA patent expired way back in the year 2000, so this isn't an issue anymore. In any case, El Gamal seems to be a perfectly fine alternative to RSA.

DSA: DSA is limited to 1024 bits, so you shouldn't use it for encryption. GPG lets you use DSA with El Gamal, using DSA for signing things and El Gamal for encryption.

For symmetric key encryption, GPG supports the following algorithms:

AES seems to be very secure. Its acronym stands for the Advanced Encryption Standard, which the U.S. government set in 2001 (it replaced DES, the Data Encryption Standard, which was considered obsolete by then). The NIST (National Institute of Science and Technology) looked at fifteen different algorithms over a five year period before choosing an algorithm called Rijndael as the winner. The four runners up were Serpent, Twofish, RC6 and MARS. All five algorithms were considered secure enough to become the new AES, but Rijndael was chosen because it had better performance on a wider variety of hardware. *Currently, the U.S. government uses AES196 and AES256 to protect top secret files, and so do many foreign governments, so that's not a bad endorsement.*

Here's an interesting fact according to the NIST: Although everyone submitting an algorithm thought theirs was the best and should win, the largest number of submitters thought Rijndael was the second best.

Twofish , which placed third in the AES competition, is *also* very secure. It's an updated verision of an earlier algorithm called Blowfish, and according to Bruce Schneier (one of Twofish's designers), there haven't been any successful attacks against Twofish yet. It isn't encumbered by any patents so it's free to use by anyone who might want to implement it, and it can be used with 128, 196, and 256 bits just like Rijndael. Here's Bruce Schneier's informational page about Twofish:

   https://www.schneier.com/twofish.html

And here's the archived page where the NIST keeps all its AES information. To see their final report, look for a PDF entitled "Report On the Development of the Advanced Encryption Standard" (the link text is "Report On the AES Selection"):

   http://csrc.nist.gov/archive/aes/index.html

Blowfish was replaced by Twofish. Use Twofish.

IDEA is the International Data Encryption Algorithm, which dates to 1991 and was an early attempt at replacing DES. It hasn't been cracked yet, and is still in use in a number of industries, but personally, I'd rather go with something like Twofish or AES.

3DES is just DES, but used to encrypt data three times. I wouldn't choose 3DES; just use something modern, like AES or Twofish. After all, DES was considered to be obsolete way back in the early nineties (IDEA was a proposal for replacing it in 1991).

CAST5 is 128-bit CAST, which was one of the earlier competitors for the AES standard. It's patent encumbered, although available without royalties, and *didn't make it to the finals for AES*, so you'll probably be a lot better off with Twofish or AES. The Canadian government uses it.

Camellia was developed by Mitsubishi and NTT, and is available in 128, 192, and 256 bit key sizes. It's patent encumbered, but available without royalties. It seems to be in use in Europe and Japan.

> ***My recommendation is to use 4096-bit RSA for public key encryption, and 256-bit AES or Twofish for symmetric encryption of files on your PC.***

So, now you have a basic idea of what encryption is about, and you know what I think about the subject, and you probably have some ideas of your own about how you want to use it. So let's get cracking, and start working with GnuPG.

Running the GnuPG GUI Provided With Gnu/Linux

You can find GnuPG's graphical user interface in the Fedora Menus. Click the "F" icon in the lower left hand corner of the screen, then the "Applications" tab, then "Utilities", then "Encryption Tool" as you can see in this screenshot:

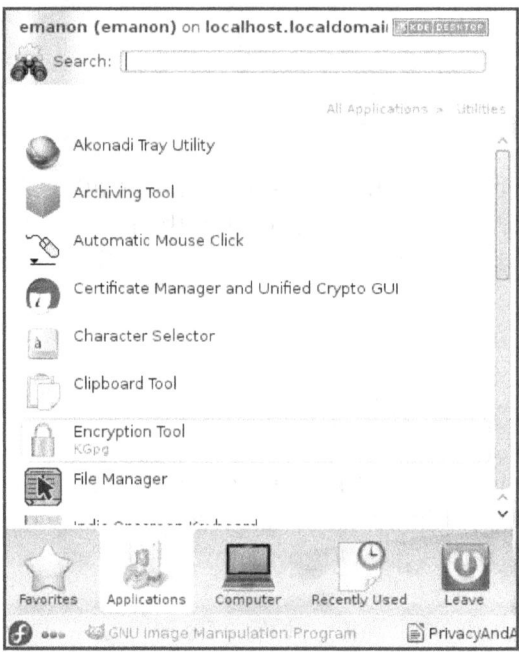

If you're using Gnome instead of KDE, you might have to hunt around for your graphical encryption tool. Instead of KGPG, which comes with KDE, you'll have a tool called "Seahorse", which by all accounts, is quite good. Learning how to use Seahorse is left as an exercise for the reader, since for me, using Gnome is *Right Out. If I were to try to express to you how much I dislike the Gnome windowing environment, it's almost certain that feelings would somewhere be hurt, bloggers would be outraged, and drama would ensue.* Let's try to bypass all that excitement. Just pay attention to what we do in KGpg, and do the equivalent thing in Seahorse, OK? I assume they're relatively similar...

Now, back on topic. The first time you run KGpg, you'll see a prompt asking you if you want to create a new secret key. Of course you do, but don't just yet. You want to see the main KGpg interface, which looks like this:

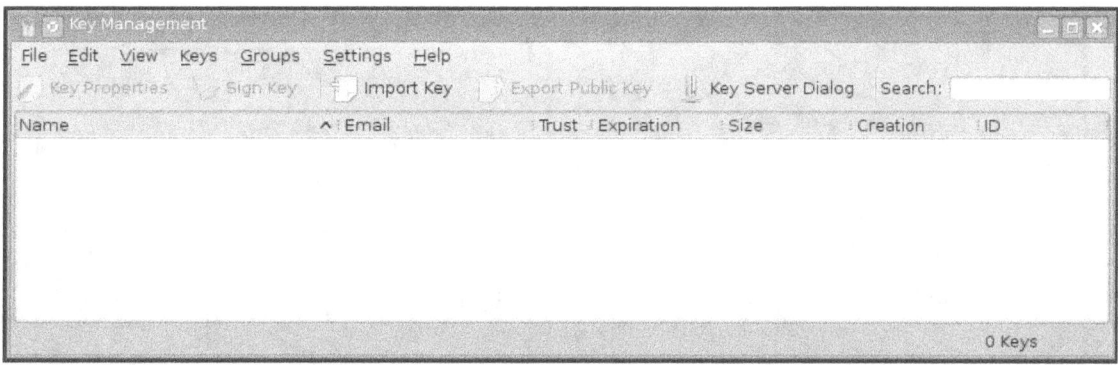

If it doesn't appear right away, you can click the tiny little gray arrow in the system tray down in the lower right hand corner of your screen and look for the KGpg padlock. Clicking the padlock will bring up the above interface. Here's what the padlock looks like, and how to find it (I've put a red circle around the little arrow you need to click):

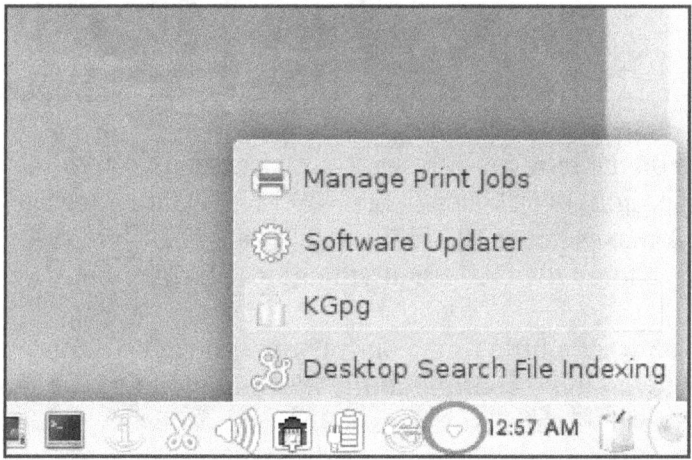

Whether you've started KGpg with the menu, or you've accessed it via the system tray, you now have access to everything GnuPG makes available to you. Unlike the weaker tools available on other operating systems, when you're using KGpg on Gnu/Linux you're flying first class. For example, the defaults available in Cryptophane for Windows users for key generation were 1024-bit DSA and up to 2048-bit El Gamal for signing and encryption, even though GnuPG on Windows allows up to 4096-bit El Gamal, and 4096-bit RSA signing and encryption. When I was setting up the examples for my Windows edition, I had to whip out the command line and do things the hard way just to get the kind of key I wanted (4096-bit RSA for signing and encrypting, or 1024-bit DSA for signing and 4096-bit ElGamal for encrypting). But with KGpg, you can choose any key strength you want, all the way up to the maximum, with no limitations and no need to go out to the command line. It's simply a better system.

So let's create a new key pair, because obviously you can't do much of anything without one. Go back to the main KGpg window, and click "Keys" then "Generate Key Pair". The key generation window that comes up looks like the following two sample images:

In the example on the left, you can see I've chosen to use 4096-bit RSA for both signing and encryption. On the right, I've chosen to use 4096-bit ElGamal for encryption and DSA for signing (although DSA maxes out at 1024 bits, so it'll be a 1024-bit DSA signing key, which is OK). There's no need to leave the GUI for anything; it's all right there, available.

Of course, if you want a little finer control, you can click "Expert Mode". This brings up a text-based session with more configurability. Nothing wrong with that, but you probably don't need it. You can see it in the first image on the next page.

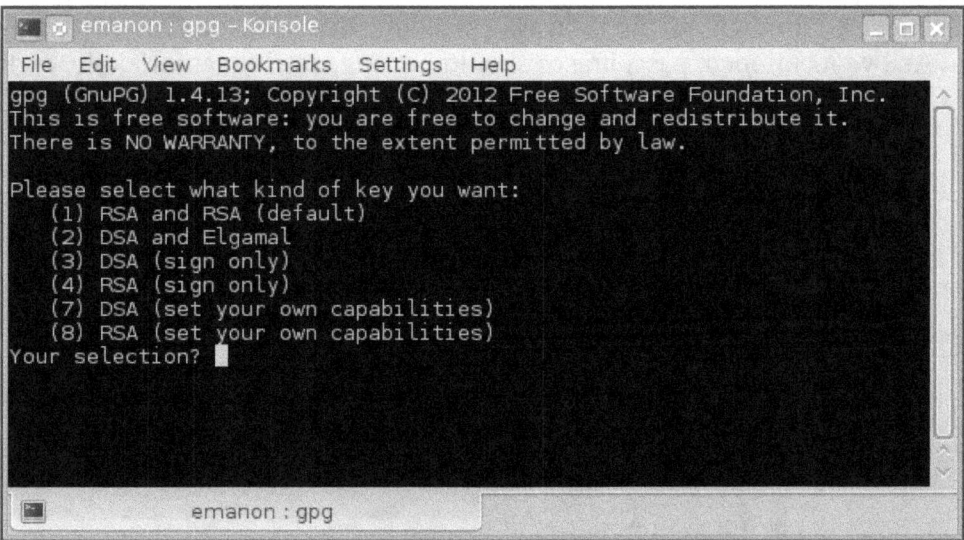

Again, you probably don't need expert mode. The graphical mode is more than sufficient. So, I'm going to go ahead and create a new key pair for 4096-bit RSA (signing and encrypting) and another key pair for 4096-bit ElGamal (encryption) with 1024-bit DSA (signing). With two key pairs, I can show you how to encrypt messages to send to other people and how to decrypt them as well. This will also come in handy during the email encryption chapter. I'll start with the RSA key set. I enter my name and email address, and set the example key to expire in three days, as follows:

Clicking "OK" brought up the following window, which allowed me to enter a passphrase. As I've mentioned, passphrases should be long, easily memorizable, and difficult to guess. I chose something fairly literary and obscure.

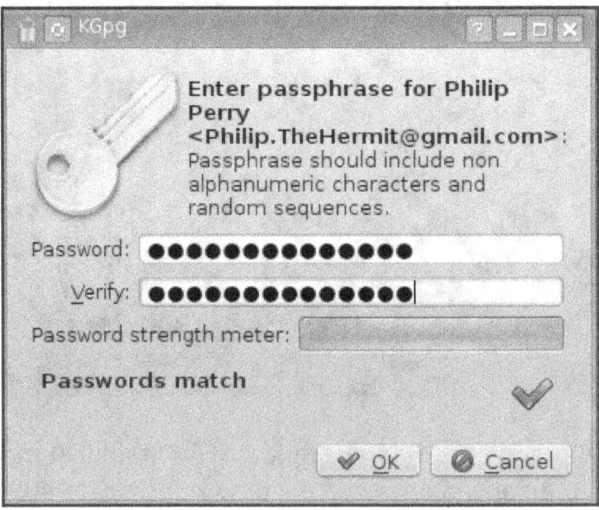

When I clicked "OK", the window disappeared and a spinning indicator appeared in the KGpg main window. After a little while, a message appeared in my system tray, which looked like this:

And the following window appeared, allowing me to set this as my default key and confirming that my key set had been created.

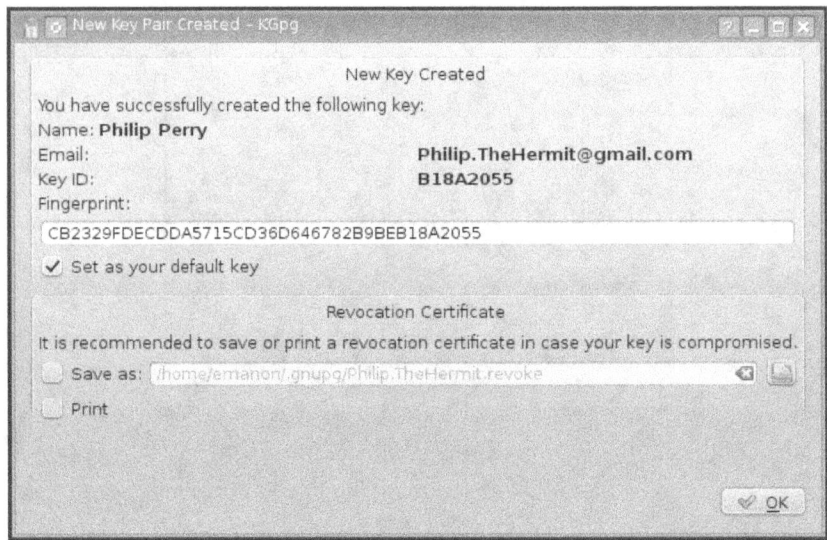

I followed the same procedure to generate my DSA/ElGamal key pair. I'll omit that process because it was identical. In the end, I could see both key pairs in my main KGpg window, as you can see in this screenshot:

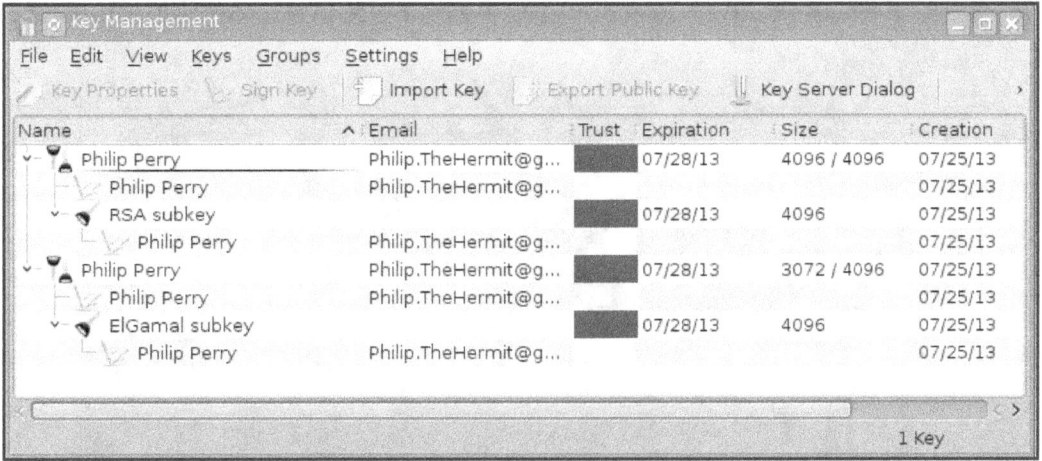

So far, so good. I've got one of each kind of key, both expire in three days (plenty of time for me to work up my examples for this book), and they're both pretty secure. Nobody's going to be able to break 4096-bit encryption within our lifetimes. If some future race of people manages to break it, we'll be long dead and it won't matter.

Our next step is to exchange public keys with someone we want to communicate with. There are two ways of doing this. The first involves exporting our public key to a keyserver where the other person can search for it. The second involves exporting our public key as a text file and emailing it to someone as a text attachment.

To export your public key to a keyserver, select one of your keys, then click "Keys", then "Export Public Key" as in the following screenshot:

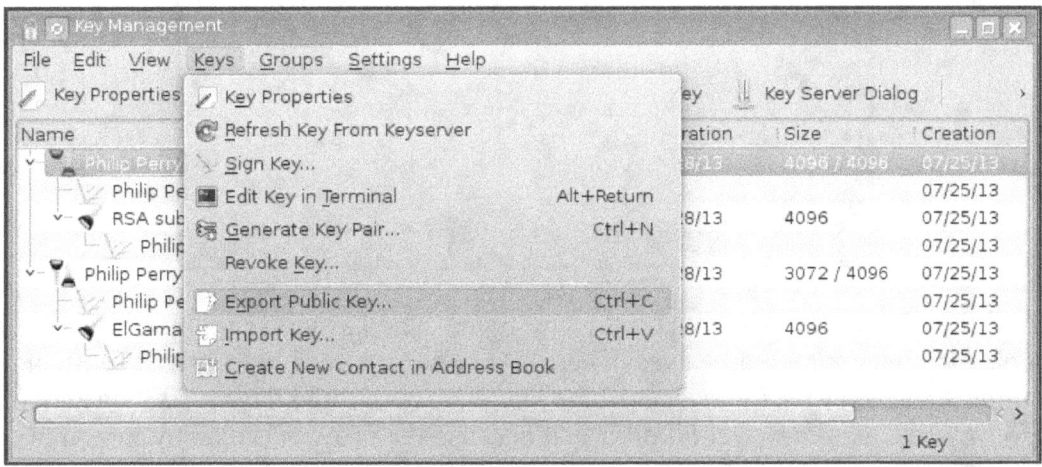

In this example, we want to export to a keyserver, so we click the radio button for

"Keyserver" and we choose a likely one from the list. Here, I've chosen keys.gnupg.net.

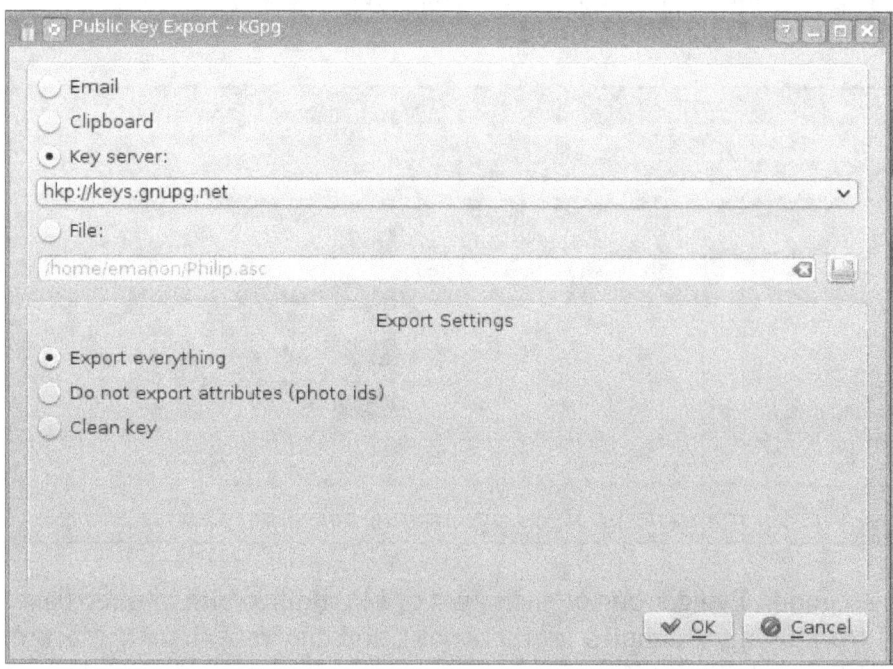

Clicking "OK" results in the following confirmation:

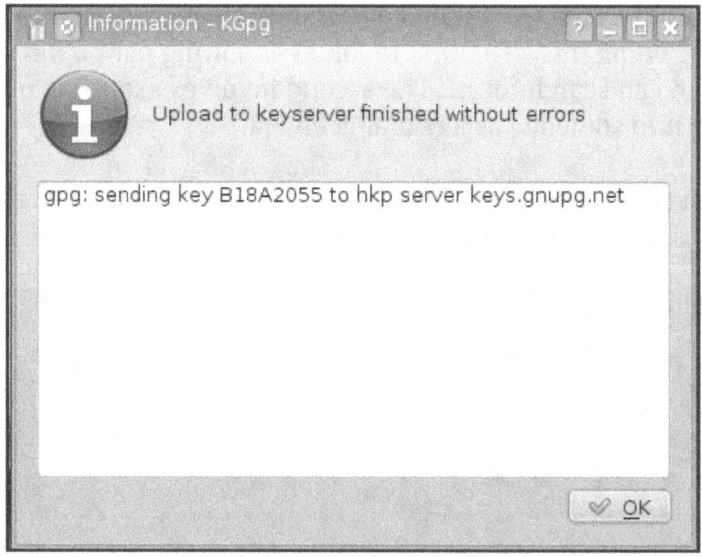

And the key is now available on the keyserver. The keyserver will pass the key to other keyservers, and pretty soon it'll be everywhere. Anyone will be able to search for it and encrypt things to send to me (at least until the key expires in three days!). I repeated this process for my El Gamal key, but I'll omit that because the process is exactly the same.

Now let's look at exporting a key so we can send it via email. This time, instead of exporting to a keyserver, we'll export it to an ASCII text file. We click "Keys" then "Export Public Key", and get the same window. This time, though, we choose "File":

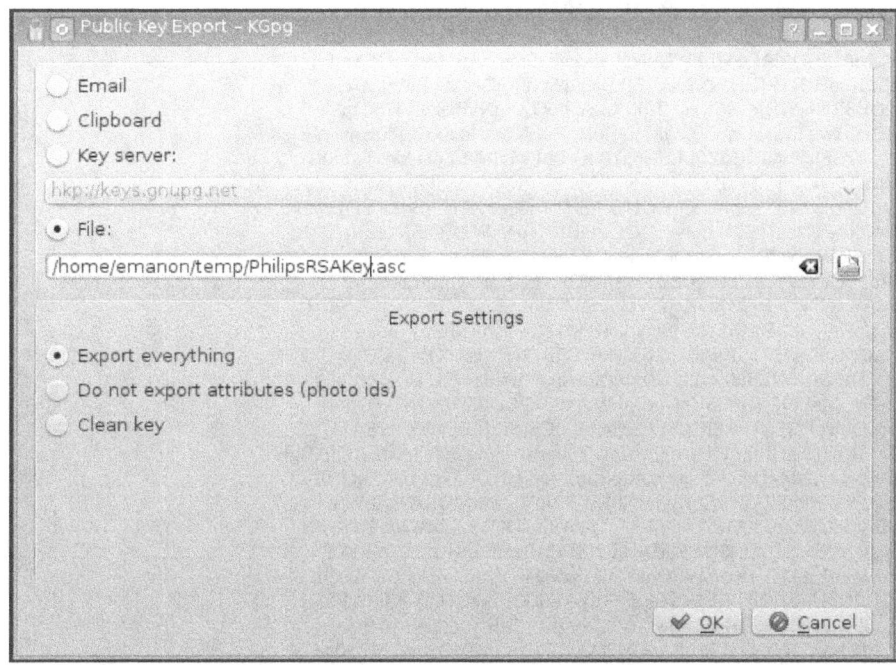

Clicking "OK" brings up the following confirmation window:

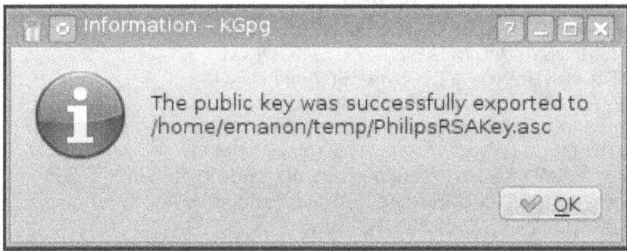

Opening the file with KWrite (a text editor) reveals that the file contains the following:

-----BEGIN PGP PUBLIC KEY BLOCK-----
Version: GnuPG v1.4.13 (GNU/Linux)

mQINBFHwuYUBEADO3NLWi7nnBkrUuVPqn65O19PkZyBA7YPN3uQ1KKXUEUWmnnBf
iMVk/jrxli28iXxfI49m4HTDXC39kQPI0P7W7r0rc3IfeL9xhAs2FhA4xUZWjuXg
vUVf6igZfLyKfPQG3tXC3RtYW9AZsLZL+V4/4NS5J4YoNLjLM4VdCjLnm9sFoNEu
n5g1Ak05j/EpZTak6iegvKs4BO57BuUwJ9o+9wrpDP6eG6C/YmI/phOUgQNehV8W
UQJKFeYNp45Uqf7U9BsxfFdx0P4k9Q4NGYSGHfnOAO3qSbPJRwTnyLNm3+mjjteS
aJ4/UPqKb2itz6iIx7h+GaPsvCB7OXS6scRnLZUMGq2Mt2mPbQzGd+wp09OOVVRz
u3fRbrzcvjERQIKmCbXM2+4myNTZSYFTlUvCFRxdqmc1b0Ex8owX0lEenlaprMg4
9IeZLyxUCDv4pg9sERUEkw7HtyKA36Rn0u4vexq2OtUuq8G+KDgBb6D8JG1I1YG5
KDZyizWXa+RvJXovq8b/WDyv7ZfVYPxCQ2Q92LWn1bvIJp2DPgDUQ8lE0lM14+8S
xMLT2Vac8eN41bkpV26cJW9ipq6s97SuxYovM5U36LKngx/YE7AOkpkv/7paxHJA
sHLEYU55D6TRT/YKMpKS0W6LyqYyXds180NGQyOVk2C+eZMv/UivKzwGjwARAQAB
tF5QaGlsaXAgUGVycnnkgKFRlc3QgUlNBL1JTQSBrZXkgZm9yIG15IExpcbnV4IGVu
Y3J5cHRpcb24gdHV0b3JpcYWwuKSA8UGhpbGlRoZUhlcm1pdEBnbWFpbC5jb20+
iQI+BBMBAgAoBQJR8LmFAhsvBQkAA/SABgsJCAcDAgYVCAIJCgsEFgIDAQIeAQIX

```
gAAKCRBngrm+sYogVWCdEACsnrcXi/HP3pN+1RKRY8BEVtFeVsd4ZIbX/7YF8WOI
sVHRQMBTvEWXqDXleRR10CfLFro9o+kmUOFIkk9hHrKB7GBrZX5H9rL+ZAzm/Cc8
wnCBCTZpa4hew2K/ZNCDg5HiyrGUKllOnUrmC2u3UEbPZSykh2kJbiezXBcP9SvD
13pHIDJGS4G4xoZ+m5x+BhMFOOzRp6qhsXfQ2/TF4pKRUc7Sx/BueQK4fJY9ew5C
m6lKAdNpqk9oXxJAbGqLOHZJIMuOKCaasO6U1+tTWu7b6DJlfG8zmS3EMyRvYcFl
v83lh4wU98JKPjN6bqXa4AJFDURdeVzm/mGSIoj5TKq0C5eRo2/sgvNoBQm66vuB
uyBycFajadM40DEd2Di/tRKjIVdAQFHLkWUdNNAIawXU9i1hloArOCofa4GFEmB5
W+4OQIqfy9ODEBCgKuoHB1zRGiHVNS9ikV7PtBHEa9YdiLuDeo10cBoxzsR7ekdV
gTmizwFgUg4cWLB9B8Rh0kYlDjqv96wxuNK0bAn2Y9loOX4gNtdIxsQK425d2px4
Z5YtYu3zcsysYGbz9pcm1wXbPs1cGnpXXZaMnQjJnBgYyEY8zsN4xbYXTslovmaW
zdxN6wah+vW9NR1j5Fz8EjaEd49DOdZ6jA2Oj6a1P/KVbbEMymN6LpDddn+FxFkF
w7kCDQRR8LmFARAAxyrC4FKdt3ceJTHGHANZ3GuoN+0KYZYDxTZt6TxSWX8MAEqL
C7NnXL/xbR1OIFlWReGR92V7Xgnbp3O55KGUQjJt5lJT+4dcg/iALgh5B4FEYQDX
NjVHVETIfgn5RMa4CjcNc8Rbe+k52Y1h0wleDCEwP8JENepNyW7VOf5MmdHnTHNf
N26nBMcLsVuM0Wo35lcWEsw7RDrjg3x+doMcrEvcYzv6UITtrJFY3ZgElzU3dlm0
UBBSsO/VScuJm8tRpS+OeYSPGXCr1U6uZfz3VlsnEd3FAEtQsq2TyoB4EoPrr5ea
uNOJQabH5y3Fy8oAA4c8//sFSa/RF2QdbKcjPWQ0FShZYepzALu0YJRCVDpCzVDH
LezxgylYEtZMi9vqfpnp7ePFuUpDiXl/Fi1Z/I8juymHHB7l1CS4XoApR9cVHcxN
Xg6IC7dyIFMCRhFzdXJG0uqeH7/z5Kv/m+uZtBQvowEJbw1vfFneM0QWVCUDqQk2
OFE1Wkpa0aggkwg37l7ek9CN5z2Bu0weUlmHmbgNBssixn5wnzl1WH75h5BkxDkB
ym94rpzwy2p6OD2rqDs5Ms190FUHrGSUqNbqgaO5oUt8EzPGdrJ308NdvjTeHvp0
HbMiDBPPrKpe0TiESQhUcRaH1sWRFRILSCCbgo66TFiC5Ie1MFEmuEZ1ry8AEQEA
AYkERAQYAQIADwUCUfC5hQIbLgUJAAP0gAIpCRBngrm+sYogVcFdIAQZAQIABgUC
UfC5hQAKCRA5PDB0sVivobMxD/0cKFqjQAuR0kKgPLhvD4KQLT1ELI5OCqQNRCTd
AmFYjdoE+Oq29AzaCXWKkIueJA8G/CqKtytplN0EWTBlnVUxchMQRB9igfbW8Poa
4SRR+8CkBFEwHSbGcLEJa2tecXvXKY00Q6E+S1QIu/C6huOQ+98lExW/RFK8u+kH
wLGmU05241ylXdSyXdCI8tzCCCzLi8GXEutQKkCN84k518keRouS+SLteNp9crYF
haJ2b6LDxfEU/XdEdjMyFLlEECVfAoxsPrBOqsNKJC3vV94rOQSGWuJfLGUmvClk
5vQ9xu6vV1A3CwiIsLIIvcUNJ24BITTAAwT88YoSbIWve6G3zm6cb1UlT2QEbkVS
h7CaaaXiMfBOXQErdMrfiYjOydHBHIEES6w5oVkG9y0w9pOtiKwa3hiKMABtS+lS
E85qLEpISqrVo1xVBr8FpdRTRYOGgk7SFdeu90D2D35VFJNqbs9TdB8RoGNYS0op
t1HZLDp6l/zAdiMYEgKvrj1B1h6/sdLWnfbtd9688S05Gybhi37DDQD4WSOroKoe
xwTwl1fUjzXRPjT4VqYtYgFZdDD/rUxjP5bWoO2KTL6bFcPgnlgfS7y0Ry6iolUr
Pcdzu1iRaHDi97PQLcaMv13fE9F87HfrYYsytWldk/2gDUzHaplmMaujpVrUI2nM
jhJiGFgCD/94Zo2WQUXPDpuMzbnQ3wC0s1w4yYPW8uGRnyYnx094Gy7pqhHiNO7W
7nR46B4Bf2YBA91bEbPXZV9MNlDlsNApmfPTLD0LwZhz3P7DvsqyVt4qmf21jJMg
DKtN1MbwyIaMSGbW/TfS/gS/uaj5VorxrOTbXvj1GfIJAnRkboioXxrGdrvyw7Cy
nETPltdlyljuAzyi4Cas1e8tkWlEXlcJ6MDuSSU/2e6sNUAYyvBP/AT5JgXBylXM
1SWK1RE6g+iOCKIopRk9ojl/icBd81Cr+8yHoVynz9YFD36viiUy5R78oFPia4kt
7FTlFO/Y+KrkIZUP3L/QY56JvSnP+felFFDqiteMrlobG7Mwv5D/aC+caJFeZpV+
eP8CiJ/zT6V7eJYDdQ1dHUNuw+oUu1sXUut1FtF/JobRiLsy9AZOY19KzucQKrde
Qo+41InRKoTeFU6rIiHOV/Sh0YlaTb1u2Ls3EGVp/QWN8vj+tBToo10R4s5TNM7d
y7zXwxWDYEcbfjSn8ZcaEsq0LCpgO+RDYYEuHrhjJYN3VOkcpacYwKhfaR8LTwlI
Wf9eQdBWDvCbDFk/7/EiZTQ9NgvkQqwB2kTI8eZM5x+k+CUlPFdGh9zmhRahFbT4
iw+eSICIHihu9t+tLygW6lN6G6njRkK8HM8bCEjwCbZxNPfJFCV0Jw==
=yWvs
-----END PGP PUBLIC KEY BLOCK-----
```

    All we have to do to give our friend our public key, then, is to email him the "asc" file containing the encrypted key we just viewed as text. So we send our buddy the "asc" file via email, and he saves it somewhere, say, a temp directory.

    Now let's look at acquiring someone else's public key so we can encrypt things to send to them. Just as there are two good ways to export a public key, there are two good ways to import one as well. The first one, obviously, is to search a keyserver for the guy's public key and download it directly.

Click "File" then "Key Server Dialog", as you can see here:

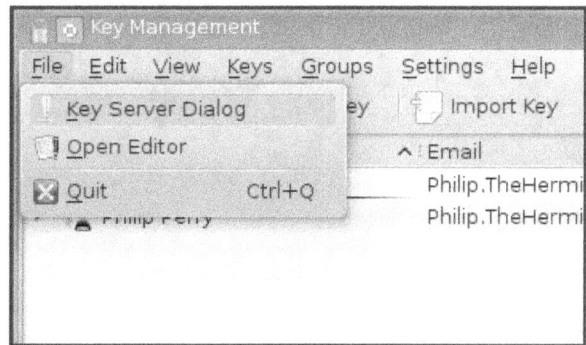

The following window will appear. You can search for a key by email address, which is probably the easiest, most accurate method. Just enter all or part of an email address, and click "Search". The Key Server Dialog will be grayed out, and a search window will appear (hopefully with results). Here, you can see I've been experimenting, and there are a number of keys associated with my email address. Sadly, I can't delete all of these because I lost their passphrase. Let this be a lesson to you: don't forget your passphrase!

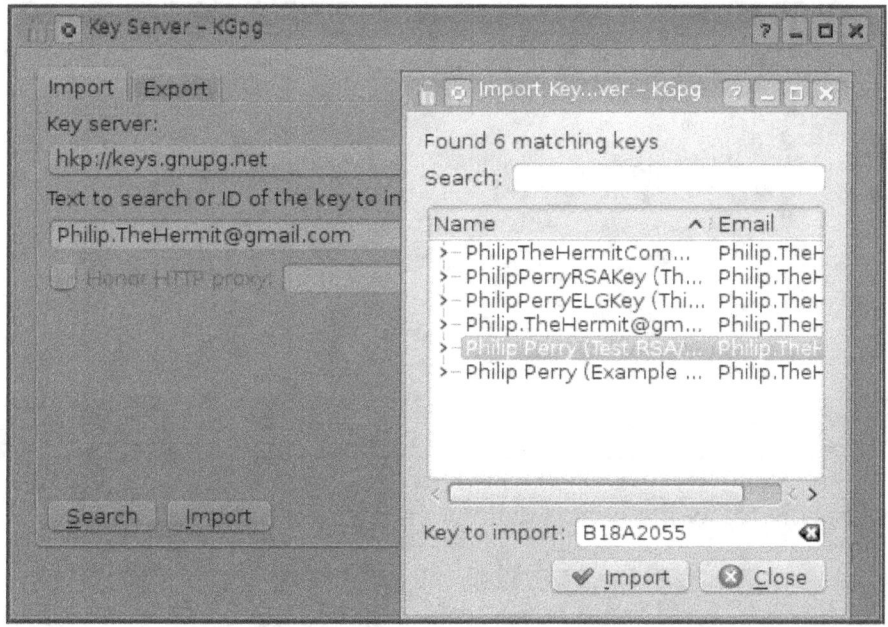

Note the fifth and sixth keys in the list. These are the keys I just created, with the three day expiration dates. I'll click the test RSA key and import it to show you what happens.

Here, since I already have this particular public key, nothing happens. GnuPG informs me that the key has been left unchanged, which is kind of anticlimactic. Well, that's OK. The only difference would be you'd see different text in the confirmation dialog.

Now, let's look at how to import a public key we've received as a text file. Remember the text file I exported earlier? Let's import it. This time, click "Keys" then "Import Key", as in the following screenshot. I suppose we could have done that a moment ago, but I wanted to show you the Key Server Dialog.

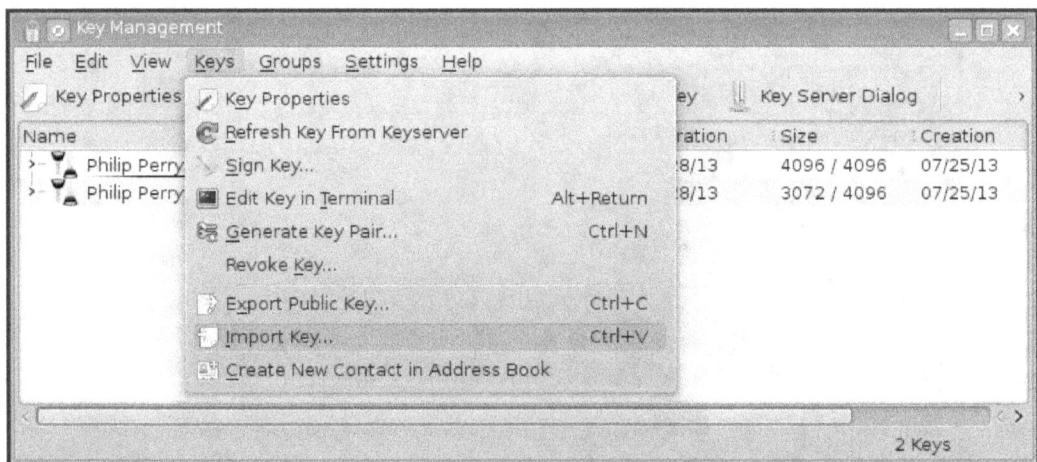

This causes the following import dialog to show up:

Note that you can manually type in a keyserver if you want, but it's a lot easier to use the Key Server Dialog and its drop-down choice of servers. Again, I'm showing you the way I like to do things; I think it's easier. Notice that you can copy the key as text to your clipboard, and use that. We're going to use the file selection dialog this time. Click the little folder button, so we can browse to our exported public key file. The following window will appear:

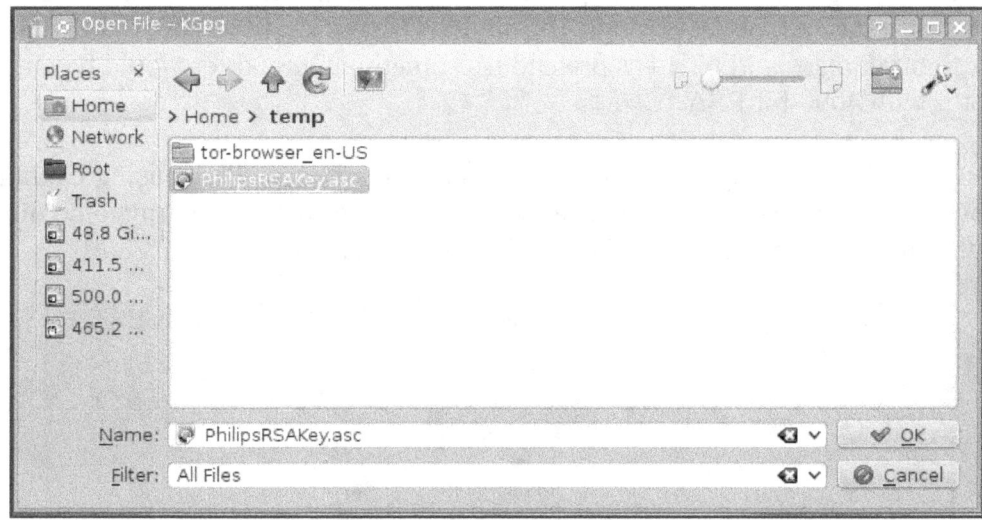

As you can see, I've navigated to my temp folder, where I've stored my exported public key. If I select it and click "OK", the previous window reappears with the file I chose selected:

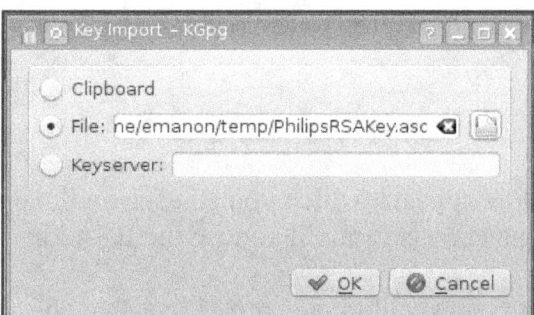

Now, if I click "OK", KGpg will try to import the selected public key. Of course, I already have this one, so I'll end up with a dialog like the one we saw earlier. Still, you get the idea. Importing keys is pretty easy.

Now that we know how to generate keys, how to export our public keys to send to other people, and how to import the public keys other people send to us, the next thing we'll want to do is actually encrypt something using a public key. Now, generally, this involves some kind of document you want to send to somebody, something with information in it you don't want other people to see. Let's say, for example, you're a whistleblower sending a PDF to a reporter. You'll probably want to encrypt the PDF and email it to the reporter using one of your anonymous email addresses through Tor, right? Of course. It's what I'd do. So I've got my Firefox tutorial, that's a PDF. Let's pretend it's something a reporter would be interested in, and encrypt it with 4096-bit RSA.

First, find the file using your regular file management tool. I'll be using Dolphin, which comes with KDE. Here, you can see I've put a copy of the PDF in my temp directory, and I've right-clicked it, then clicked "Actions", then "Encrypt File".

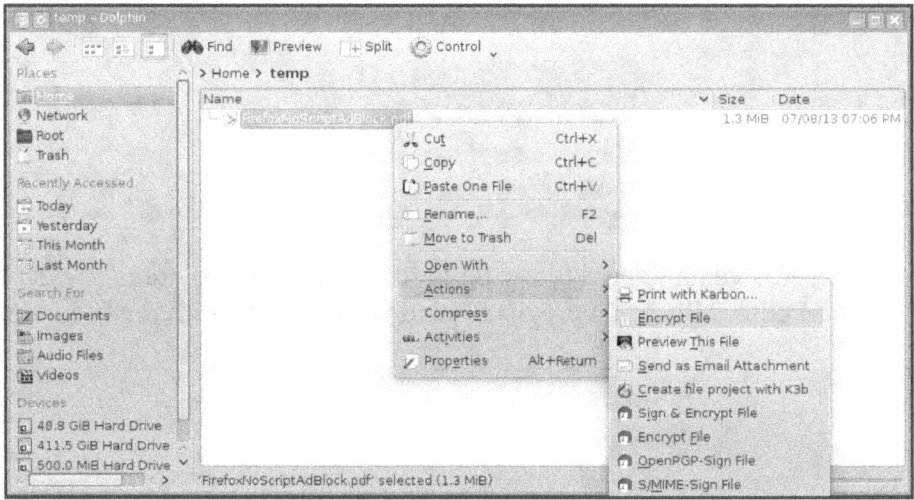

A key selection window appears, which you can see on the next page. I'll click "Options" so I can make some choices, and I'll choose the RSA key for this example.

There are a few things you should note here. First, I've checked "Allow encryption with untrusted keys", because a person you might want to communicate with might not have anybody available to vouch for his key (like me; I'm a total recluse). This is a problem with the whole concept of "web of trust" (the idea behind whether or not a key is trusted). The idea is that you can sign someone else's public key, affirming that you trust it and granting some level of trust to it. If enough people do that, a key can be considered trustworthy. The problem is that this process shuts out loners and recluses like myself. So, you know, you might want to be willing to encrypt to an untrusted key. Not everybody is an academic with a bunch of grad students, just hanging around waiting to trust his keys. Just saying.

The next thing you should notice is that I'm using "ASCII Armored Encryption" which converts the encrypted file from a binary file to an ASCII file, which makes it less likely to get garbled in transit. This is always a good thing, so I generally select this option.

Note also the option for "Symmetrical Encryption". Don't set that; I've had some trouble getting it to work. Stick to public key encryption while using the GUI, and you'll be fine.

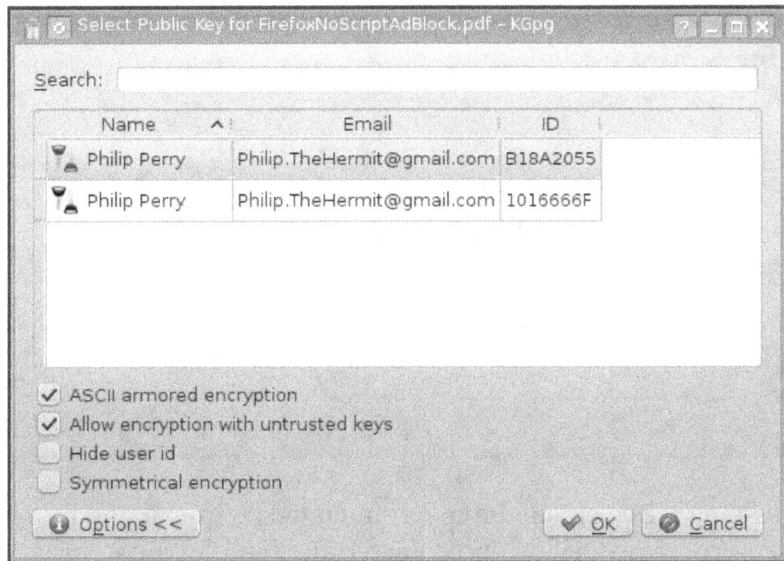

Clicking "OK" causes KGpg to encrypt the file using the selected public key. This produces an "asc" file (since we chose ASCII armoring) which is slightly larger than the source file. If we didn't ASCII armor the file, the extension would have been "gpg".

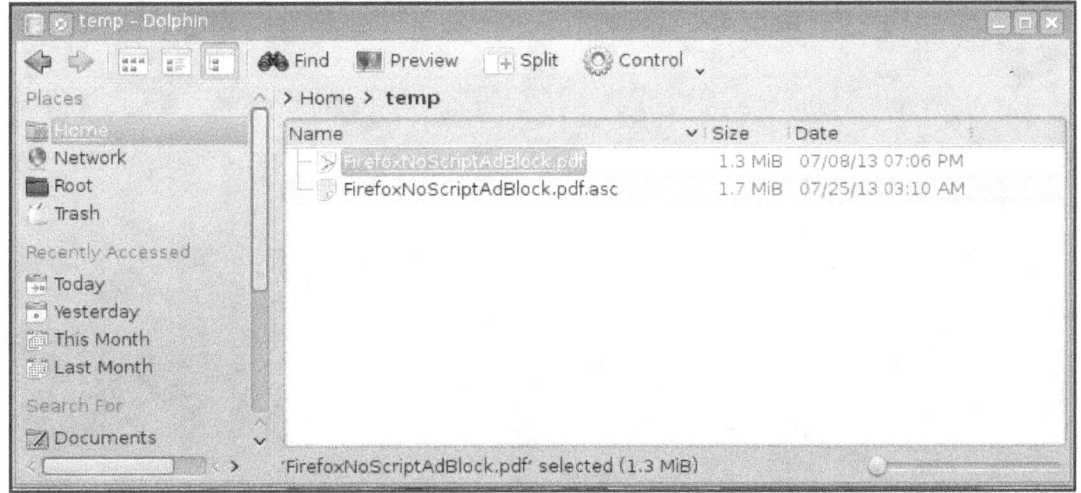

And there you have it. We've encrypted a file using 4096-bit RSA. We can email this file to our friend, who will be able to decrypt it using his secret key. Let's see what's in the file; since it's an ASCII file, we can open it up in KWrite.

As you can see in this screenshot, it's a big block of encrypted data, just like the public key we exported earlier.

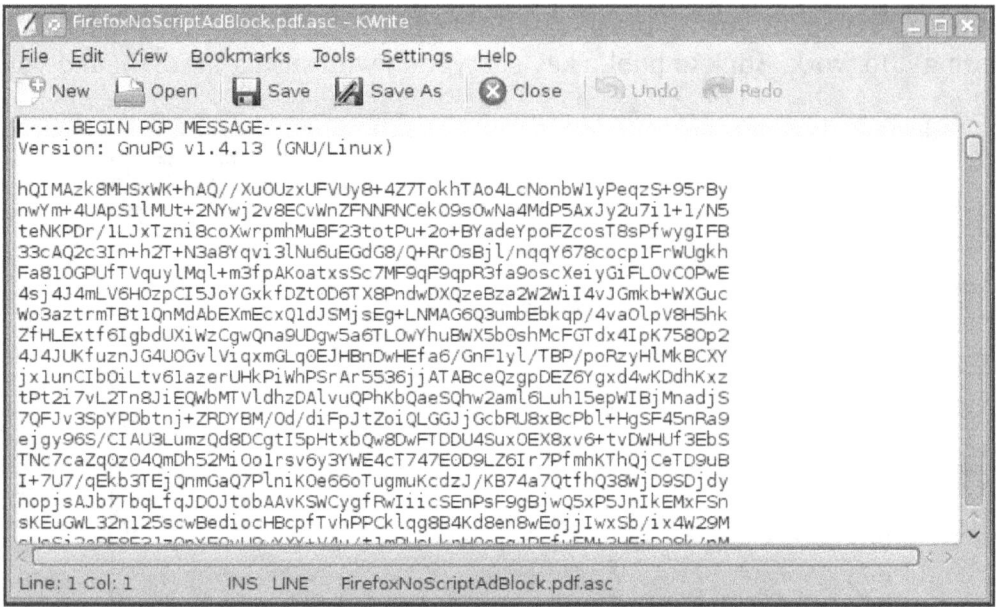

Now, let's assume we've emailed it to our intended recipient, and he's got his copy of KGpg ready to go. Here's how he'll go about decrypting the file. First, he'll right-click the file, then he'll click "Open with KGpg" as you can see here:

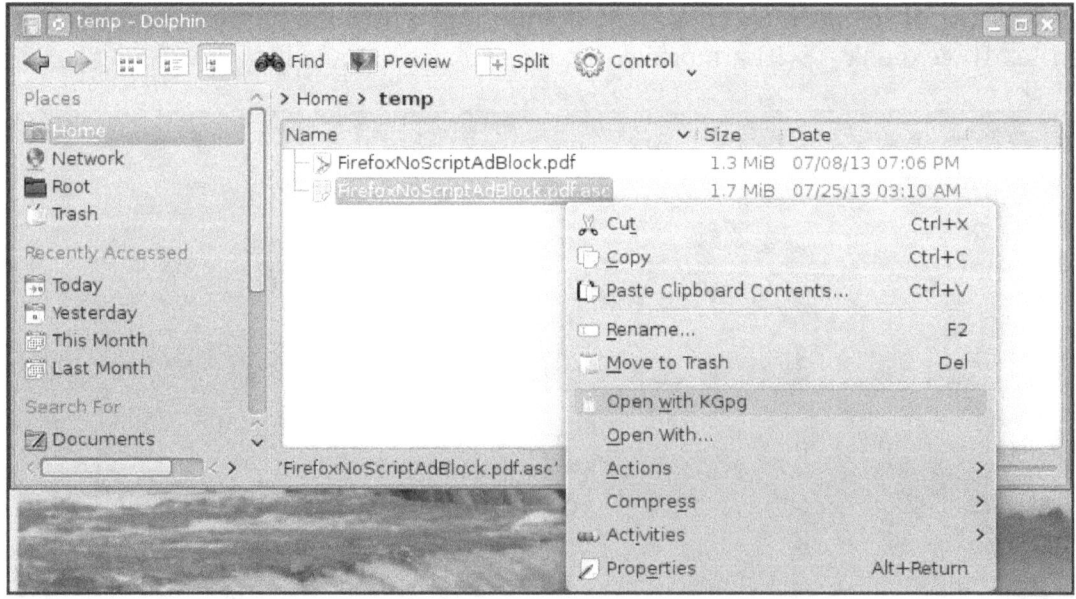

This brings up the following window, which asks for a passphrase.

Entering the correct passphrase and clicking "OK" will result in the file being decrypted, as so:

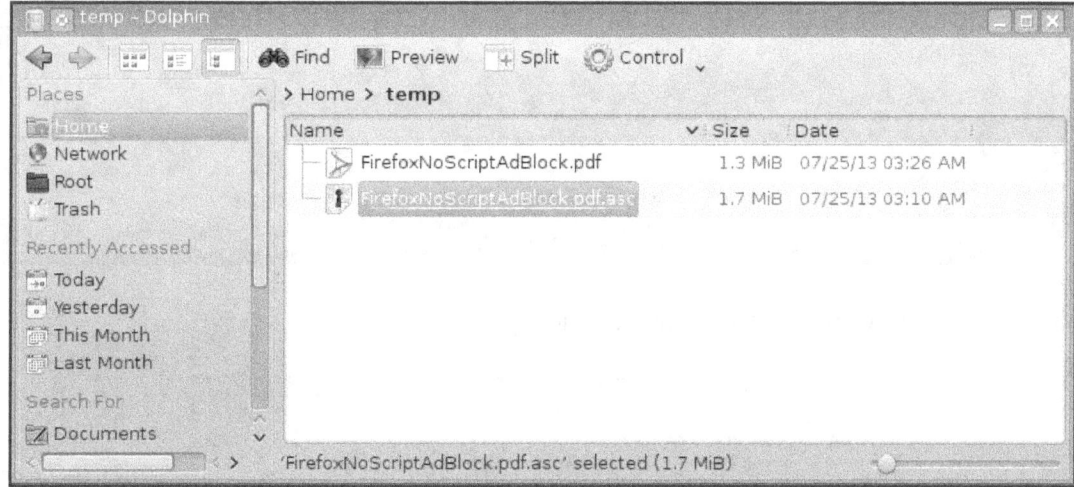

So far, we know how to generate key pairs, we know how to upload our public keys to keyservers and mail them to our friends, we know how to import the public keys other people send to us, and we know how to encrypt and decrypt files using our key pairs. Now let's get a little fancier, and both encrypt and digitally sign the things we want to send.

Signing and Encrypting Files With Kleopatra

KDE offers a nice tool called Kleopatra, which you can use to do more complicated things with encryption, like both signing and encrypting a file. Let's do that next. We'll encrypt the PDF we've been playing with using my ElGamal key, and we'll sign it with my RSA key. Then we'll decrypt it and verify the signature, so we can tell that it really came from me and not some nefarious third party. Sound interesting? Let's get started.

Just as we did before, we locate the file we want to encrypt, we right-click it, and we click "Actions". But this time, we click the Kleopatra link "Sign and Encrypt File", as in this screenshot:

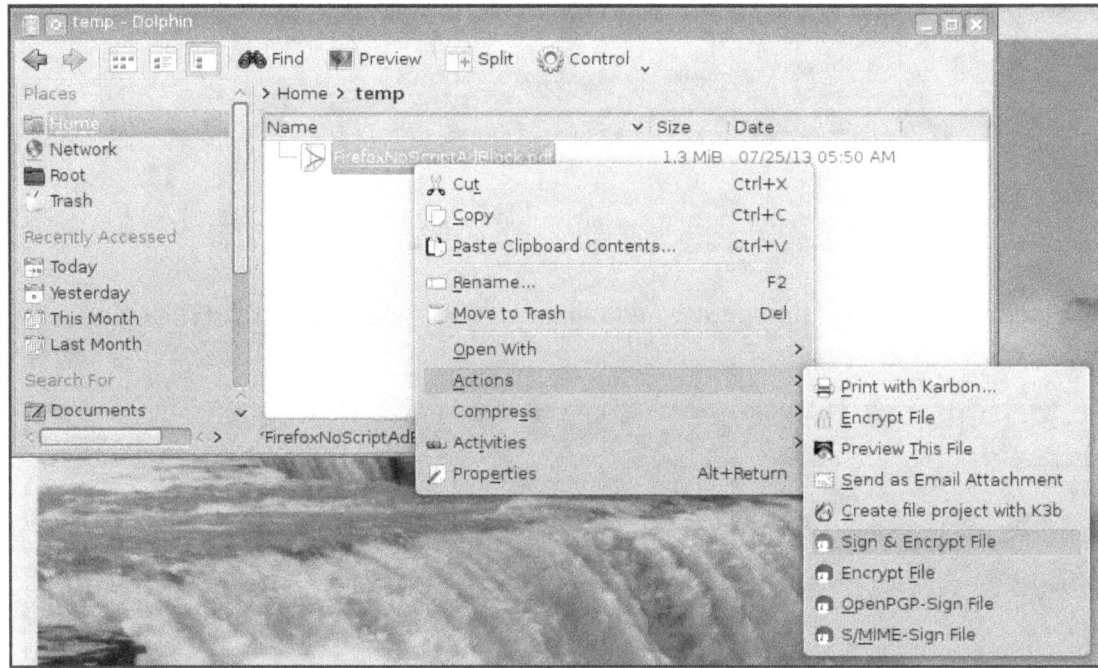

Kleopatra shows us the following window:

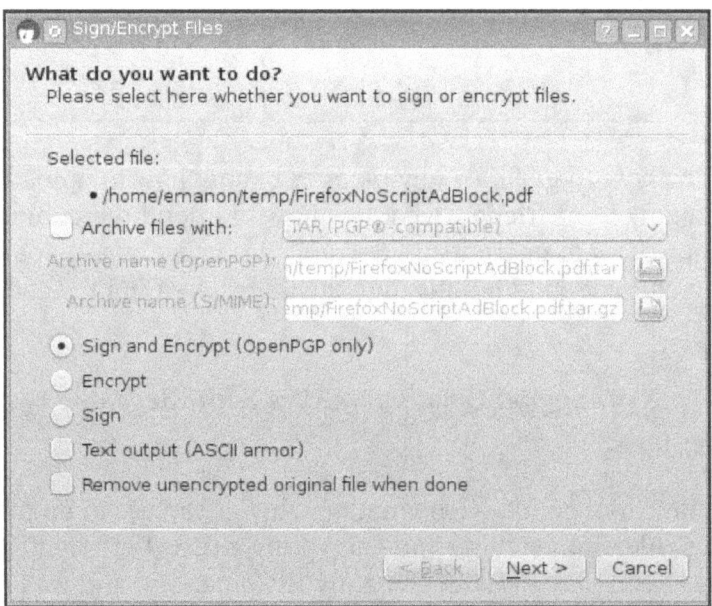

Since we want to sign and encrypt, we select "Sign and Encrypt". Don't worry about the OpenPGP only blurb; GnuPG is OpenPGP compatible. It's not a problem. Note that you can also decide to remove the original file when you're done, which can come in handy. Finally, we can ASCII armor our output, although for this example I've skipped that (so you can see a file with a gpg extension on it for a change). Clicking "Next" shows you this window, where I've chosen to encrypt for my El Gamal key:

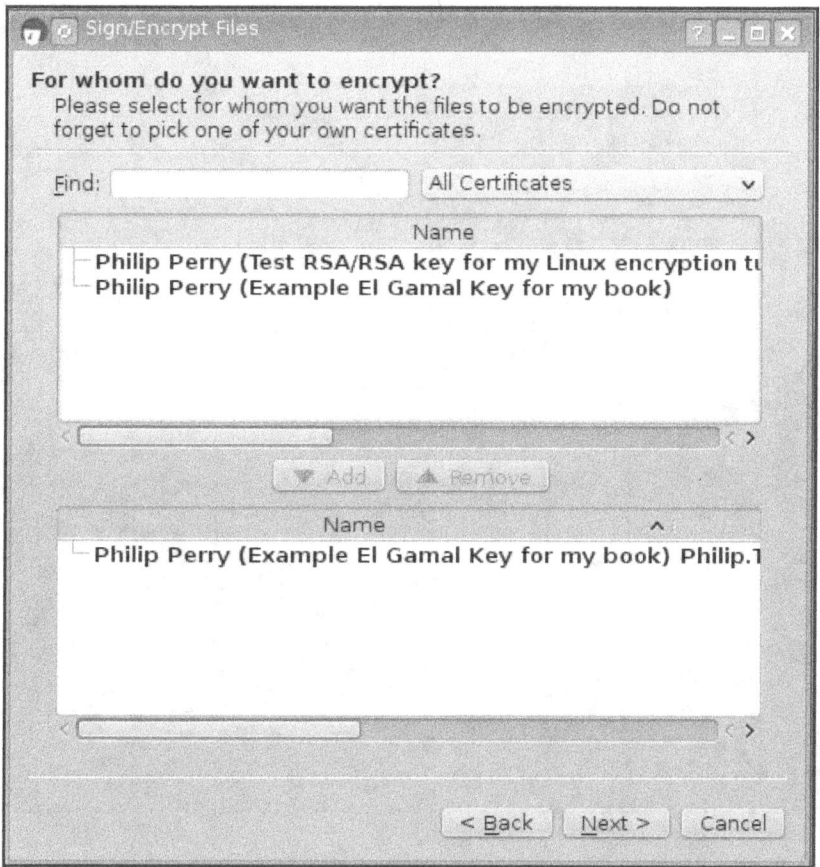

Clicking "Next" brings you to the following window, where you choose the key you'll sign the message with.

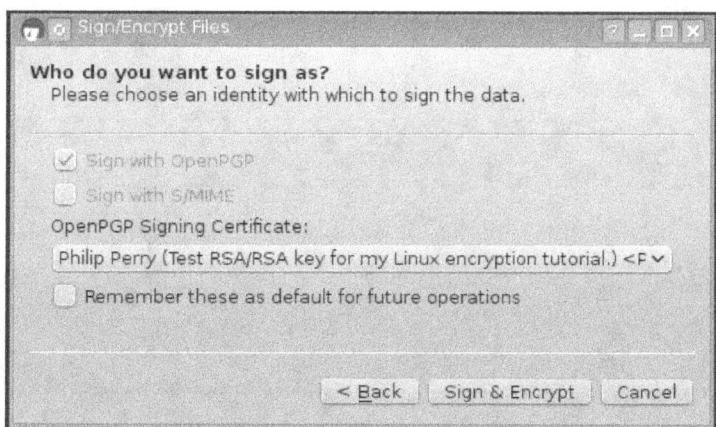

Finally, clicking "Sign & Encrypt" brings up a window which asks you for your passphrase, so you can sign the encrypted file with your secret key. It also brings up a results window, so you can see whether the encryption was successful. Here you can see the two windows side by side:

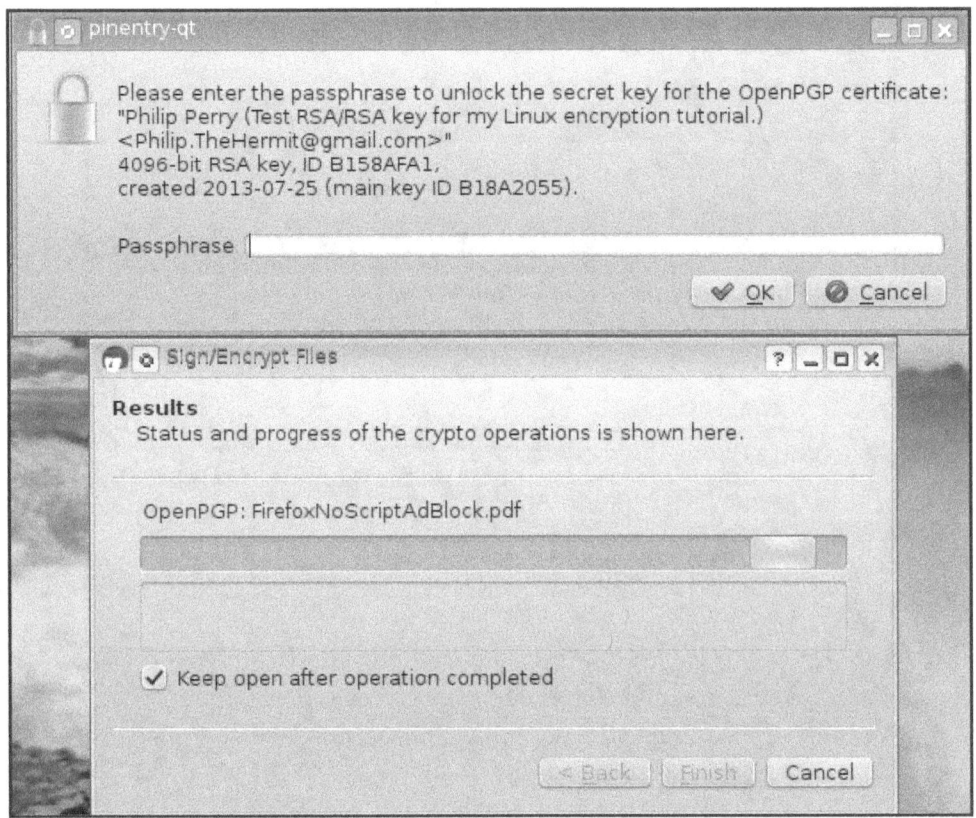

Here's the final window, after the file has successfully been encrypted:

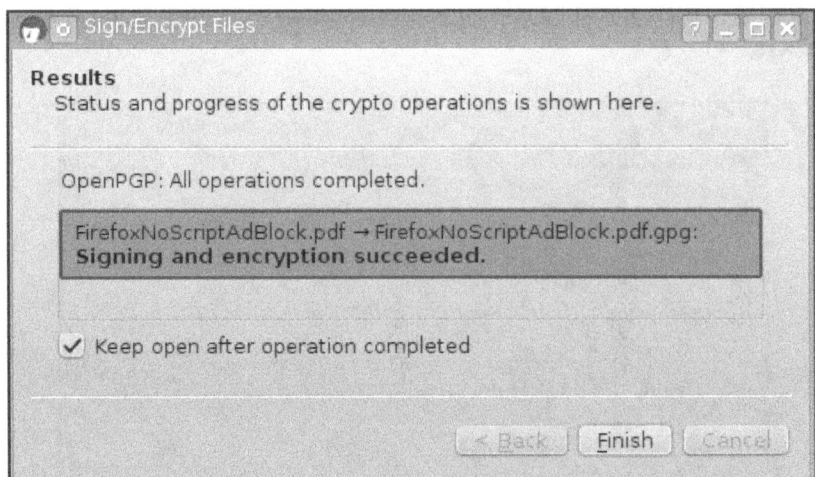

So, that's how you sign and encrypt a file. Now let's look at how you decrypt and

Protecting Your Privacy and Anonymity Online   Gnu/Linux Edition

verify a signature. We'll be using Kleopatra for this as well.

First, find the encrypted file you want to decrypt and verify. Right-click it, then click "Actions", then "Decrypt/Verify File", as in this screenshot:

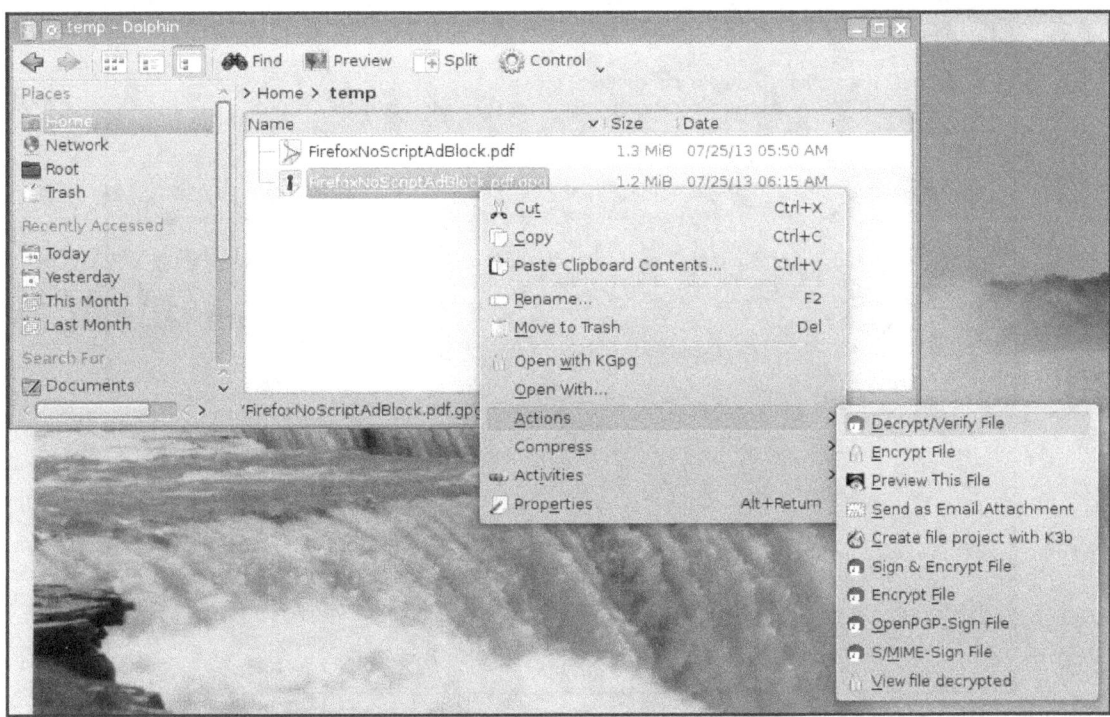

This brings up the Decrypt/Verify window, which appears like this:

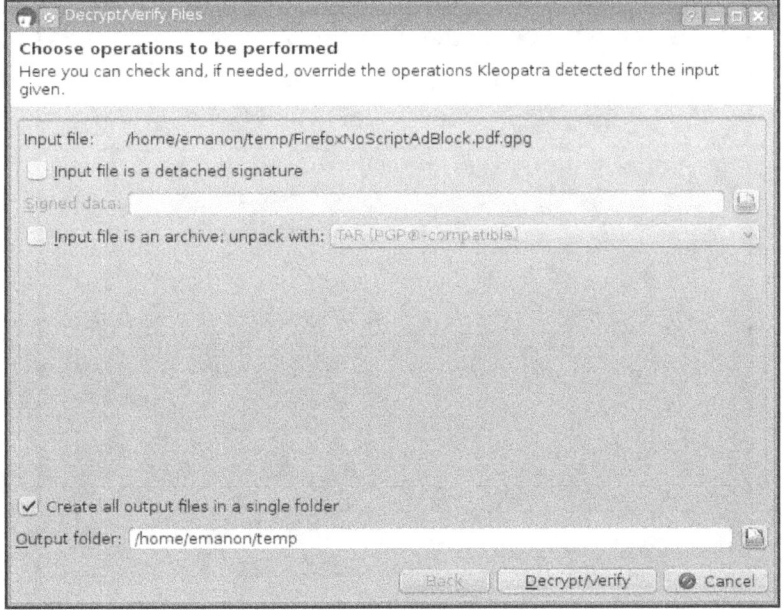

Page 61

I generally don't change any of the defaults on the Decrypt/Verify window. I just click "Decrypt/Verify, which brings up a request for the passphrase for the key the file was encrypted for (in this case, my ElGamal key). Here's what that looks like:

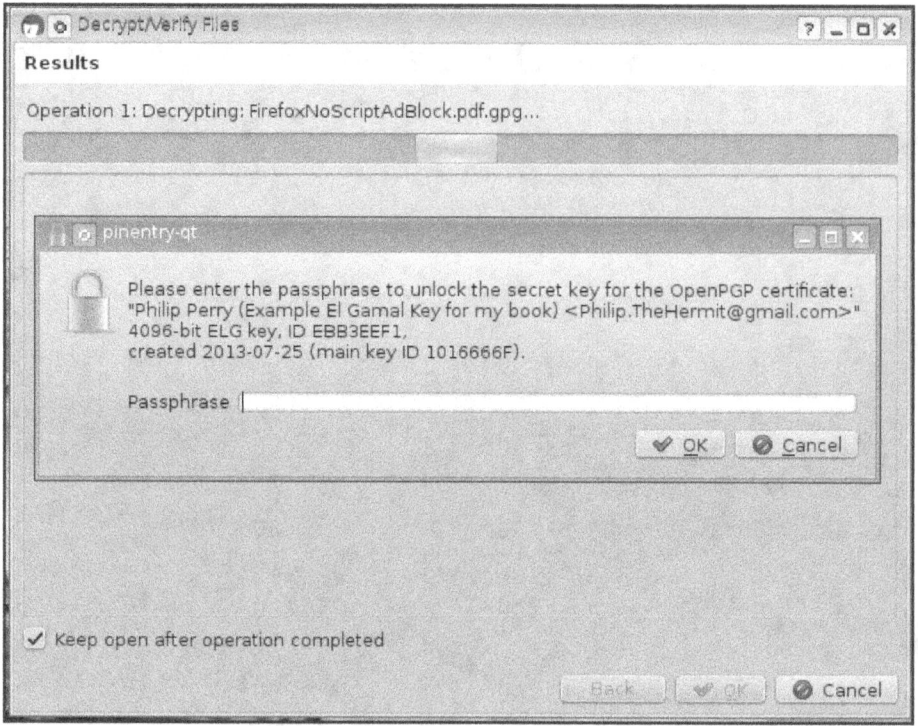

And the final window, indicating that we successfully decrypted and verified the file, looks like this:

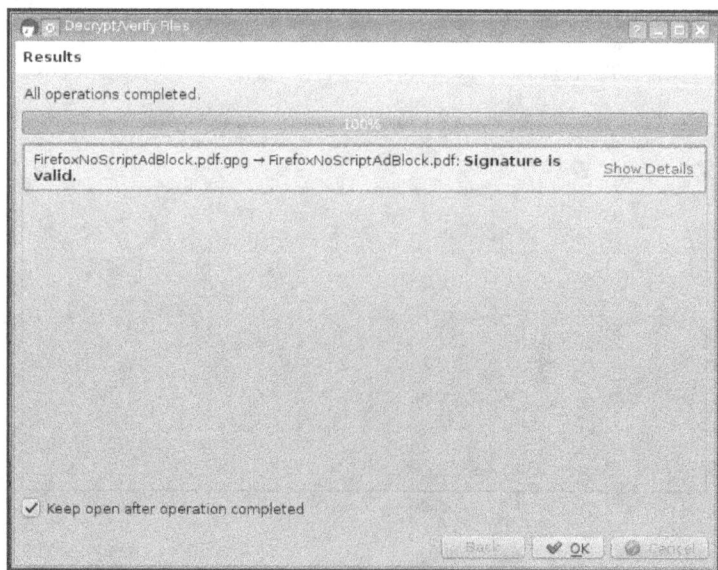

So that pretty much covers public key encryption, at least giving you enough information to do all the important stuff. Of course, we've barely scratched the surface, but you can read the rest in the manuals for the various pieces of software we've been using.

Using Symmetric Encryption to Protect Your OWN Files

We're going to get into a little deeper water here, because we want to have more control over what's going on. The first thing we're going to want to do is adjust the GnuPG configuration file so it chooses more secure encryption methods over less secure ones. Specifically, we're going to add the following lines, expressing a preference about the order in which GnuPG selects encryption methods. These are lines from my configuration file, by the way. You can find yours in your home directory, in "*.gnupg/gpg.conf*". Note that the first line is word-wrapped; it's actually just a very long line. Don't put the carriage return in. Copy these lines somewhere between the comments at the top of the file and the first settings in the file, so they're easy to find.

```
# ======================================================================
# HERE ARE MY DEFAULT PREFERENCES -- BY PHIL
# ======================================================================
default-preference-list AES256 AES192 AES TWOFISH 3DES CAST5 BLOWFISH MD5 SHA512 SHA384 SHA256 SHA1 BZIP2 ZLIB ZIP Uncompressed
personal-cipher-preferences AES256 AES192 AES TWOFISH BLOWFISH CAST5 3DES
personal-digest-preferences SHA512 SHA384 SHA256 MD5
personal-compress-preferences BZIP2 ZLIB ZIP Uncompressed
# ======================================================================
```

The important thing to note here is that for personal-cipher-preferences, I prefer AES256 first, then AES192, then AES, then TWOFISH, and only then the rest. When I'm encrypting, if I don't otherwise specify a preference, I'll get AES256. But we have to test this, if we want to be sure. So let's encrypt something with symmetric encryption, but first, two cautionary notes:

> *Note #1: Unlike with public key encryption, I had some difficulty getting symmetric key encryption to work using the graphical tools (i.e. right-clicking a file in the file manager). Maybe it's a bug, maybe I'm doing something wrong, but going to the command line seemed to solve the problem completely. So for the symmetrical encryption portion of this chapter, we're going to use the command line tools instead of the graphical ones.*
>
> *Note #2: The pass phrase for a symmetrically encrypted file is very important: it's the only thing protecting your data, so you have to choose something long enough and obscure enough that nobody will be able to guess it. However, it <u>also</u> has to be something you can memorize and accurately type back in later. Obscure poetry works, and so do random movie quotes, song lyrics, etc. Don't write your pass phrase down! Memorize it, and don't tell it to anyone.*

Have a look at the command line session below. It illustrates the three important commands you'll need for symmetrically encrypting files. The first thing I did was see what encryption methods were available, using the command "***gpg --version***".

Next, I encrypted a PDF using symmetric encryption with the command "***gpg --symmetric FirefoxNoScriptAdBlock.pdf***". (I had to supply a passphrase).

Finally, because I wanted to make sure I was encrypting with AES256, I used the command "***gpg --list-packets FirefoxNoScriptAdBlock.pdf.gpg***". This is a debugging trick, and using it I can see what encryption method was used. It seems my configuration file was set up properly, because the method used was indeed AES256.

Here's the text of the session in a more readable format, with blank lines added between commands and results. In the following, my commands are in **_highlighted bold italic_**, and the system's prompts and responses are in *plain italic*. In the print version of this book, the colors won't show up because it'll be in grayscale, but hopefully the contrast will still make it easier to tell one from the other.

[emanon@localhost temp]$ ***ls***

FirefoxNoScriptAdBlock.pdf

[emanon@localhost temp]$ ***gpg --version***

gpg (GnuPG) 1.4.13
Copyright (C) 2012 Free Software Foundation, Inc.
License GPLv3+: GNU GPL version 3 or later <http://gnu.org/licenses/gpl.html>
This is free software: you are free to change and redistribute it.
There is NO WARRANTY, to the extent permitted by law.

Home: ~/.gnupg
Supported algorithms:
Pubkey: RSA, RSA-E, RSA-S, ELG-E, DSA
Cipher: IDEA, 3DES, CAST5, BLOWFISH, AES, AES192, AES256, TWOFISH,
*   CAMELLIA128, CAMELLIA192, CAMELLIA256*
Hash: MD5, SHA1, RIPEMD160, SHA256, SHA384, SHA512, SHA224
Compression: Uncompressed, ZIP, ZLIB, BZIP2

[emanon@localhost temp]$ ***gpg --symmetric FirefoxNoScriptAdBlock.pdf***

(Here I was asked for a passphrase)

[emanon@localhost temp]$ ***ls***

FirefoxNoScriptAdBlock.pdf FirefoxNoScriptAdBlock.pdf.gpg

[emanon@localhost temp]$ ***gpg --list-packets FirefoxNoScriptAdBlock.pdf.gpg***

:symkey enc packet: version 4, cipher 9, s2k 3, hash 2
*   salt 22bab6f43285700d, count 65536 (96)*
gpg: AES256 encrypted data
:encrypted data packet:
*   length: unknown*
*   mdc_method: 2*
gpg: encrypted with 1 passphrase
:compressed packet: algo=3
:literal data packet:
*   mode b (62), created 1374739447, name="FirefoxNoScriptAdBlock.pdf",*
*   raw data: 1366176 bytes*

[emanon@localhost temp]$

Ok, so now we've checked to see what encryption methods are available in our copy of GnuPG; we've also symmetrically encrypted a file, and verified that we're using the algorithm we wanted to use, AES256. *Now, we'd like to decrypt it.* Since we're using a command line approach, we'll decrypt it that way too. The command we need is simply
"**gpg FirefoxNoScriptAdBlock.pdf.gpg**", as you can see in the below screenshot. It asked me for my passphrase, which I entered, and since the source file was still there, GnuPG asked whether we should overwrite it, and I said "y".

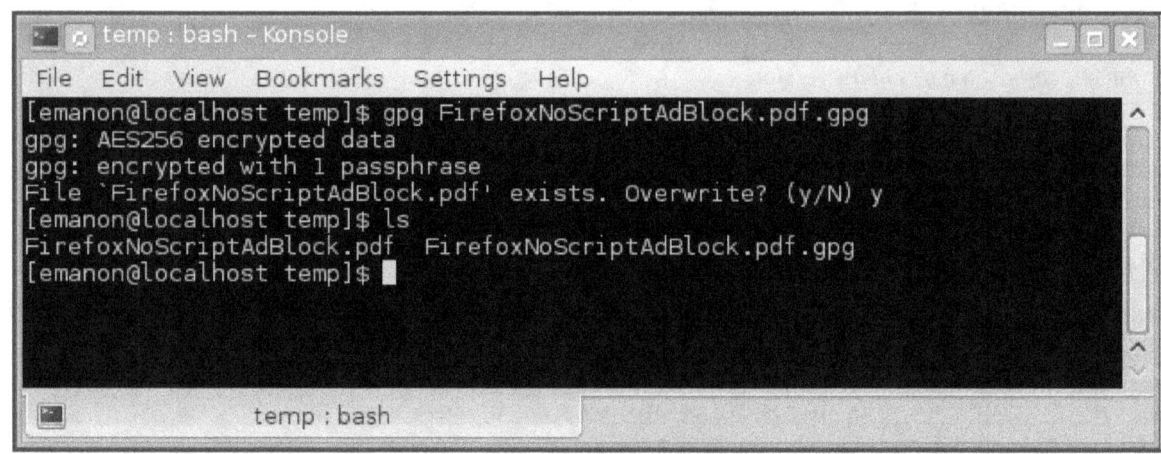

Here's the text in color-coded format, as before, with my commands in **highlighted bold italic** and text from the system in *plain italic*;

[emanon@localhost temp]$ ***gpg FirefoxNoScriptAdBlock.pdf.gpg***

(Here I was asked for a passphrase)

gpg: AES256 encrypted data
gpg: encrypted with 1 passphrase
File `FirefoxNoScriptAdBlock.pdf' exists. Overwrite? (y/N) ***y***

[emanon@localhost temp]$ ***ls***

FirefoxNoScriptAdBlock.pdf FirefoxNoScriptAdBlock.pdf.gpg

[emanon@localhost temp]$

Similarly, if we want to decrypt the file, we can do this graphically by right-clicking on the encrypted file, then clicking "Open with Kgpg", as you can see here. This seems to work with no problems.

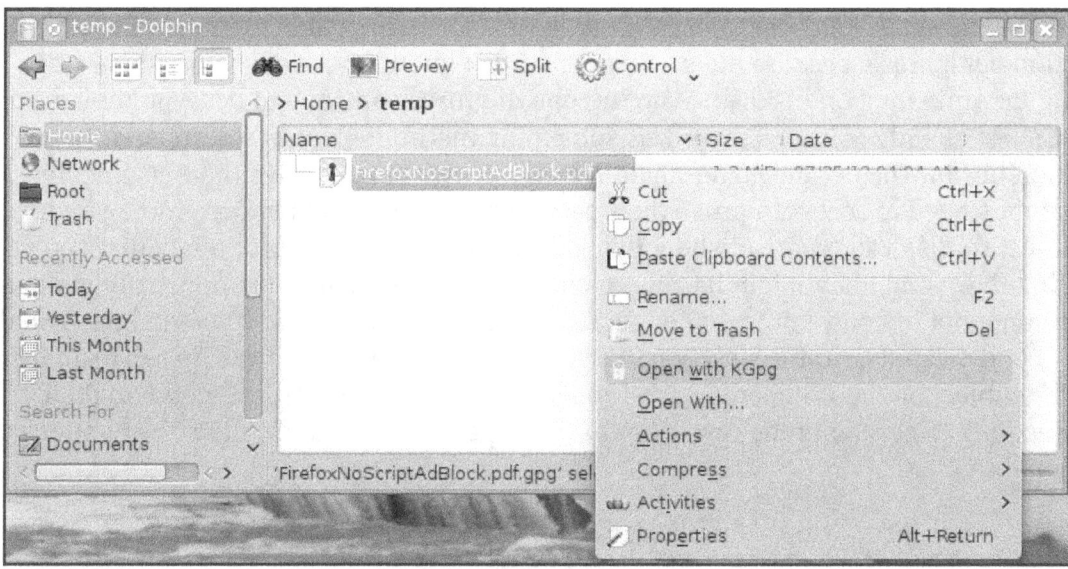

Doing so brings up the following window, asking us for our passphrase:

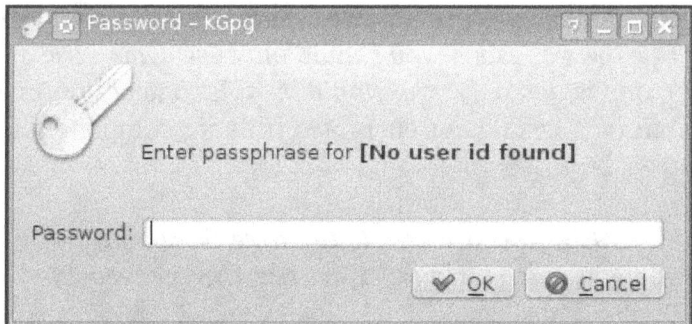

Of course, there's no user id because we encrypted symmetrically, which doesn't use a pre-existing key. Entering a passphrase (the "password" they're asking for) and clicking "OK" results in the source file being decrypted and made available.

That's pretty much all there is to symmetric encryption and decryption. If you take the time to read the GnuPG manuals, you can probably get a lot more fancy than what I've shown you, but realistically, you probably won't need to. It's pretty easy, and pretty secure.

There's one more thing I'd like to discuss before we move on to the email chapter.

Two Things to Keep In Mind:

One Supreme Court decision recently held that a man couldn't be forced to give up his encryption passphrase, because the government didn't know for sure whether there was anything incriminating on his disk. Another one did force someone to decrypt her hard drive, because she'd already admitted there was something incriminating on it. Apparently the distinction lies in whether the government already knows or can prove there's something on a disk that they need to access to prove their case. The courts won't let them force you to decrypt just so they can go on a fishing expedition, but if they know for a fact that you've got something they want, they might be able to compel you to give it to them, usually via jailing you for contempt of court until you cooperate. Of course, I'm not a lawyer, and this is only my layman's understanding of the situation, based on what I've read online. There's a good article about the subject on the Wikipedia page for "Key disclosure law" (scroll down to the United States section). Read about the cases that have happened so far, and follow the citations to get more detail:

https://en.wikipedia.org/wiki/Key_disclosure_law

Next, *remember not to use symmetric encryption for things you want to send to other people.* The fact that it's protected only with a pass phrase becomes a weakness the minute more than one person needs to know the phrase. The phrase could be intercepted by a third party, or your friend could foolishly write it down where someone could see it, or something else could go wrong. *For these reasons, you should only use symmetric encryption for things that belong only to you, and which only you should be able to access.* As long as your pass phrase only exists in your own head, your encrypted files are completely secure.

Using Secure Delete to Make Sure Your
Unencrypted Original Files are Unreceoverable

Here's an issue which is relatively easy to deal with on Gnu/Linux systems, but a bit more difficult on other, more proprietary systems. Let's say you've encrypted a file. If someone gets their hands on it, they can't read it because they don't know your passphrase, right? But if they've gotten their hands on your laptop, not only do they have your encrypted file, they've got your unencrypted source file too. Clearly, if you want to be secure you've got to get rid of the original file.

Merely deleting the file is insufficient, because as long as the file's space on disk hasn't been overwritten yet the file can still be recovered. It can often be partially recovered even if it's been overwritten. What we need to do is not just delete the file, but overwrite its disk storage dozens of times with random data so it's no longer recoverable.

The command-line tool that comes pre-installed on Gnu/Linux is called *"shred"*. This tool overwrites a file three times with random patterns, and you can supply an additional command line parameter to add a final pass to overwrite the file with zeroes. You can supply a different parameter to change the number of passes shred does, which you'll want to do since three passes isn't really enough these days. **Shred** is *mostly* good enough, but being a fairly paranoid guy I like to go a little further.

A better tool in my opinion (also command-line) is *"srm"*, aka *"secure remove"*, which you can install by searching for *"srm"* in the Fedora software repository. **Srm** by default carries out the Gutman method for deleting fies, which involves 35 passes over the data with different patterns calculated by Gutman's research to most effectively obscure the data. Gutman theorized that since low frequency magnetic fields penetrated deeper into the recording media, writing a higher-frequency field over the top can still leave traces behind. Different manufacturers encode their drives in different ways, so different patterns of data are better for obscuring data on different types of drives. So his method alternates numbers of different patterns designed to deal with all the different ways drives are encoded, covering all the different possibilities and making sure the data is actually obscured. Doing it this way makes a file you've deleted completely unrecoverable, even for an adversary with near-infinite resources (like a government or large corporation). This is a thing of beauty.

To use **srm**, whenever you have to securely delete a file, open up a command line session, **cd** to the directory your file is in, and use **srm** instead of the normal utility **rm**. Because it's writing over the file with so many patterns, it takes a little while (the more data there is, the longer it takes) so be patient. In particular, whenever you encrypt a file or when you're done with a file you've temporarily decrypted, use **srm** to get rid of the plain-text file safely (leaving only the encrypted file). **Srm** works on directories as well, just like **rm**, and offers the same parameters as **rm** (like **-rf**).

While we're on this topic, there's another neat tool available called *"sfill"*. This tool is similar to srm, but what it does is overwrite empty space. For example, if you run it on a directory, it overwrites all the empty space associated with that directory so nothing that was ever stored in it can be recovered. You can run sfill on an entire hard disk if you want, although be aware, that takes many hours, particularly for large hard disks. Anyway, install it and play around with it a little. You'll like it.

NOTE: When you're deleting from thumbdrives (or any other type of solid state device), first you'll want to use **srm** to delete any files you want to get rid of, and then you'll want to use **sfill** to clear out all free space on the whole thumbdrive. This is because thumbdrives move files around to prevent individual memory elements from wearing out. Deleting a file, even securely, might not get rid of all the recoverable copies on the thumbdrive. *So, make sure you use both tools to cover all the bases.* Unfortunately, this will increase wear and tear on the thumbdrive and shorten its operating life somewhat. It can't be helped, and it's definitely worth it.

Use Fedora's Hard Disk Encryption Feature

One final recommendation: Encrypt your entire hard disk. Fedora allows you to encrypt your entire hard drive, including the system partition, when you initially install Fedora. This way, you cannot boot the computer or access it at all unless you're able to supply its encryption passphrase. This offers three incredibly important benefits:

* Nobody will be able to sneak into your house or apartment and fire up your computer to look at your files when you're not around.

* Nobody will be able to sneak into your house or apartment and fire up your computer to install evil things like keyloggers or spy software when you're not around. (Well... They might have to resort to a hardware-based one, but you have a better chance of spotting that.)

* If someone steals or confiscates your computer, who cares? It's encrypted.

Remember to pick a nice, long passphrase (something appropriately weird and literary, perhaps). Don't write it down, and don't tell it to anybody. Matter of fact, don't even mention to anyone that you've encrypted your hard disks. Let it be a surprise for the person trying to mess with your computer. People love surprises!

This concludes my introduction to encryption. You'll want to learn more on your own, so work your way through the various manuals of the tools we've gone over. There's way too much material to cover in a little tutorial like this, enough to keep you busy for a long while. It's interesting stuff, too.

Chapter 4:

Encrypting Your Email With Thunderbird and Enigmail

So far, we've looked at anonymous web browsing with the Tor Browser, the use of anonymous webmail and forum accounts, and the use of strong encryption to protect your personal files and send secure messages as encrypted email attachments. Now, let's look at how you can secure your non-anonymous email accounts -- the ones you use day to day with family and friends. Note that since your day-to-day email *isn't anonymous*, your ISP and the government will be aware that you're having an encrypted conversation, and they'll know who you're conversing with. Should you care? Maybe, maybe not. The question is, can anyone persecute you because you're having a given conversation? The answer to this question should tell you which of the following two approaches you'll want to use:

Two Approaches to Encrypted Email:

__Non-Paranoid Approach:__ If you're __not worried__ about people knowing that you're talking to someone, and all you want is to prevent third parties from eavesdropping on you, you don't have to go to great lengths to protect your communications. All you have to do is use the approach described in this chapter. It's easy, doesn't require a lot of work, and it's pretty secure. This approach is good for things like lawyer-client conversations, talking to fellow protesters when you don't care who knows you're protesting, and private conversations with family and friends. Remember: "they" will know you're talking, but they won't know what you're saying. This is more than enough most of the time.

__Paranoid Approach:__ Sometimes you don't want __anyone__ to know you're having an encrypted conversation. Perhaps you're a whistleblower in the U.S. government (and you know they'll merrily ruin your entire life if they figure out who you are). Maybe you're working as an anti-corporate activist, and you don't want the company dragging you into court to ruin your life. Maybe you're trying to blow the whistle on some kind of criminal activity you've found out about, and you don't want any criminals coming around at midnight to talk about it. Times like these, you'll want to be a little more careful:

> *a) Keep all source material (like your typed messages, etc) on a thumbdrive, not on your computer itself, so you can get rid of it if you have to. Never store it or anything related to it on your actual computer. Note: thumbdrives are better than external hard disks, because they're much easier to destroy or get rid of.*
>
> *b) Encrypt your messages using at <u>least</u> 2048-bit RSA or El Gamal, and the public key of the recipient. Store the encrypted file on the thumbdrive as well. Don't sign the file!*
>
> *c) Start Tor, and within the Tor Browser, log into an anonymous email account you've created for this specific purpose, which you'll use only to communicate with your recipient.*
>
> *d) While still in Tor, send the encrypted file as an attachment using the anonymous email account.*
>
> *e) Hide or destroy the thumbdrive. Hammers work pretty well, and so does fire.*
>
> *f) Delete the recipient's public key from GnuPG. You can always download it again if you have to. Remember to do so within Tor!*
>
> *g) Don't tell ANYBODY what you're up to, and don't admit to anyone that you're the one who sent the material, even if a reporter (for example) promises to protect you as a confidential source. Loose lips sink ships.*

Now that we've got that out of the way, let's look at using the non-paranoid approach to secure our non-anonymous email. Securing your non-anonymous email involves the following steps:

1. Making sure your email client is configured to use SSL or TLS to encrypt its connection to the email server. If it isn't, or if your provider doesn't support this, your passwords can be seen in plaintext as they're transmitted from your PC to your email provider. Admins at your ISP can see them, and if you're on Wi-Fi, so can hackers hanging out at the cafe providing your Wi-Fi connection. (Of course, if they're running an intercepting proxy, they might be able to see them anyway -- be careful with Wi-Fi!)
2. Configuring your email client to remove all messages from the server, storing them only on your PC. This way, they're not sitting around waiting to be read by anyone with admin access.
3. Setting up a whitelist on your email client to sort incoming emails from people and businesses you know, moving them automatically to specific local folders. Emails from people you don't know will be moved to a "To Be Determined" folder so you

can quickly scan through them, pull out anything good, and delete the rest in a couple of mouse clicks. Finally, you'll have a rule for marking anything that wasn't addressed directly to you as spam (since spammers tend to use BCC lists a lot).
4. Finally, you'll want to configure your email client to use GnuPG encryption, so you can send encrypted and signed emails to people. A good email client offers tools for this.

Let's get started. We'll begin by downloading and installing **_Mozilla Thunderbird_**, an email client I think is probably the best available. Then we'll look at how to use encryption with it.

Acquiring and Installing Thunderbird

Because you're using Gnu/Linux, your life has once again been made easy; you can get Thunderbird from Fedora's software repositories. Start up the software repository (Apper), and do a search for "Thunderbird". You should see something like this:

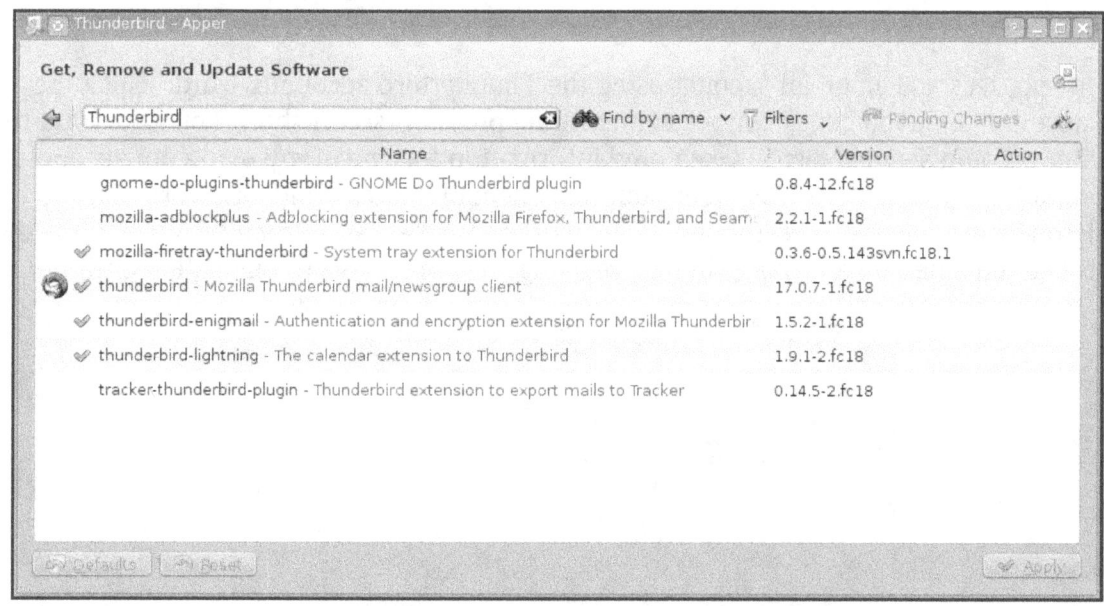

As you can see, I've already got the packages you're going to want to install. They're Thunderbird itself, the thunderbird-enigmail package which handles encryption, thunderbird-lightning which handles calendar functions (nothing to do with this book, I just like it), and the Mozilla firetray for Thunderbird (which pops up "You've got mail" type messages, which can be useful).

So, alright, select all four of those and click "Apply" at the lower right to install them. It takes a minute or so, and then it's done; you've already got everything. Now you just have to learn a few things you can do with it. From here on in, everything works approximately the same on all platforms. In the next image, you can see the main Thunderbird interface. Here, I've clicked the options button to show you where it is (it looks like three horizontal bars, in the upper right hand corner -- I've circled it in red). Take a minute to look around and see where everything is.

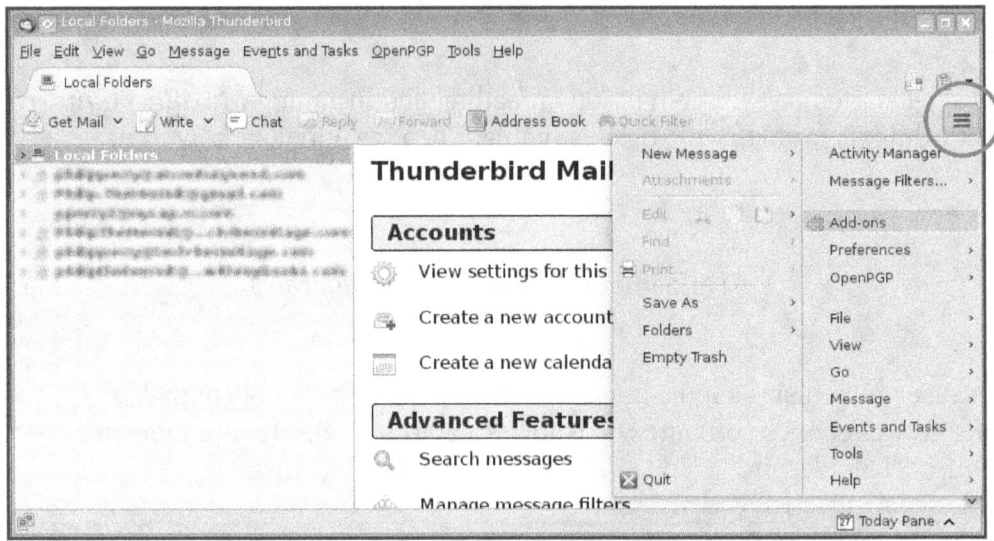

Next, let's add an email account using the Thunderbird account wizard. Click the "Add a new account" link you can see in the center of the previous screenshot. This takes you to the following account setup screen (I've entered information for one of my mail.com accounts as an example). As you can see, you enter your name, email address, and password and Thunderbird goes out and finds the rest. This works for most large email providers; however, if you've set up email on a hosting site you're using, you may have to manually configure it.

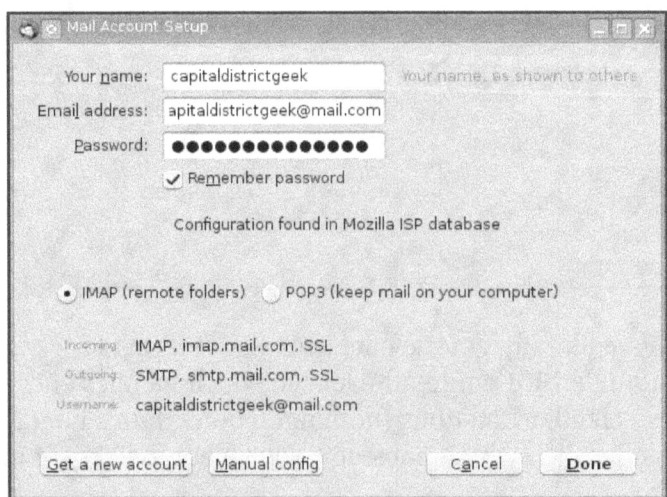

If you have to manually configure your account, you'll need to find out a few things from your email provider. Usually, they'll have a FAQ or a help site about connection settings, and this should be relatively easy to find on their home page. Just look around for a tech support link, and find their FAQ. The specific settings you're looking for are:

1. Their POP3 or IMAP site. If the email provider is (for example) example.com, the POP3 site should be pop.example.com, or pop3.example.com. If it's IMAP, it'll be more generic, like mail.example.com.
2. The port you need to connect to (it should be something like 995 for an SSL-encrypted connection. If they want you to use 110, they're probably not encrypting your connection, and you should find a new provider).
3. The SMTP site you should use for sending email. For example.com, the SMTP site should be smtp.example.com.
4. The port to use for SMTP. If they're encrypting the connection, this port should be something like 465, or 2525. If it's 25, they're probably not encrypting and you should find a new provider.

In the next screenshot you can see a manual configuration of the same email provider I set up in the previous screenshot. You can see it's not that complicated.

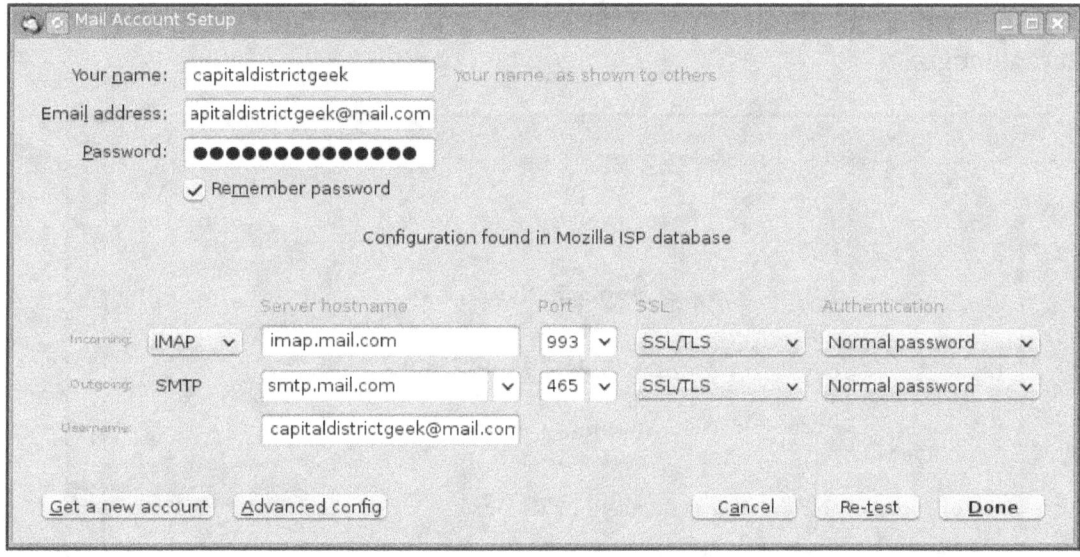

I was a little concerned about the "Normal password" Authentication, but it was connecting over SSL, so I wasn't terribly concerned about it. Basically, there are just a number of different levels of password security you can have if you're running an email server, and most providers default to "Normal password". Obviously it'd be a lot better if providers would encrypt their passwords, and only store the encrypted hashes, but what can you do... Clicking "Done" will set up your account and return you to the Thunderbird main window.

The next thing we want to do is set up encryption, and integration with GnuPG. To do that, we go back to the Options button, and this time, we click "Add-ons". This opens up a new tab in Thunderbird that shows Thunderbird's add-ons site. Here's the Options drop-down, showing the Add-ons link (I've highlighted the link):

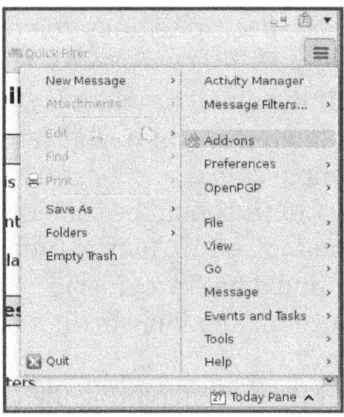

Clicking the link takes you to the Thunderbird Add-ons site, where you can work with plugins. Since we're using Gnu/Linux, we've already installed Enigmail, so we don't have to hunt for it. We can go straight to configuring it. Click the "Extensions" tab on the left hand side of the Add-ons Manager. You should see something like the below screensot. Note that since we're on Gnu/Linux, and GnuPG and Enigmail were installed from the software repository, everything should already be set up and ready to go. Click "Preferences" just to make sure, though.

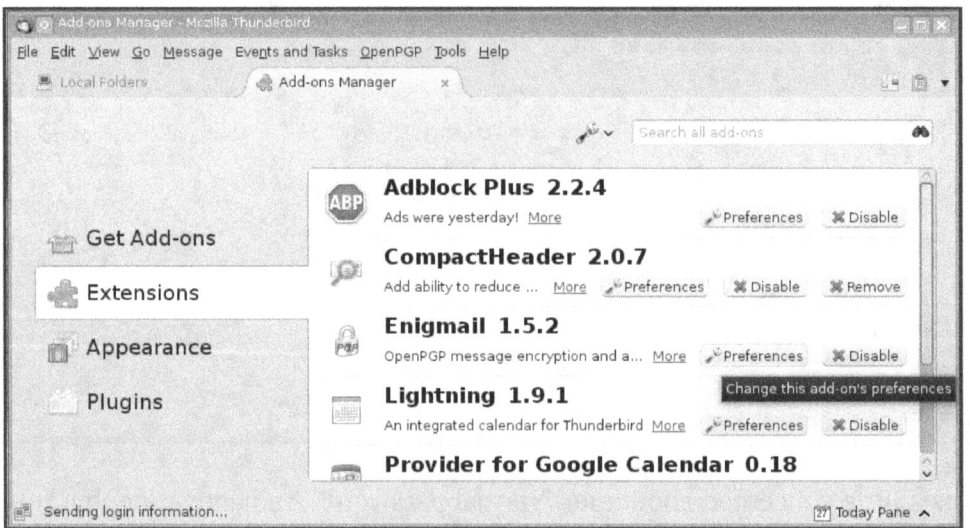

On the next page, you can see that Enigmail doesn't yet know where to find GnuPG, which is a bit of a problem. So, check the "Override" checkbox, and click the "Browse" button so we can track down the GnuPG binary.

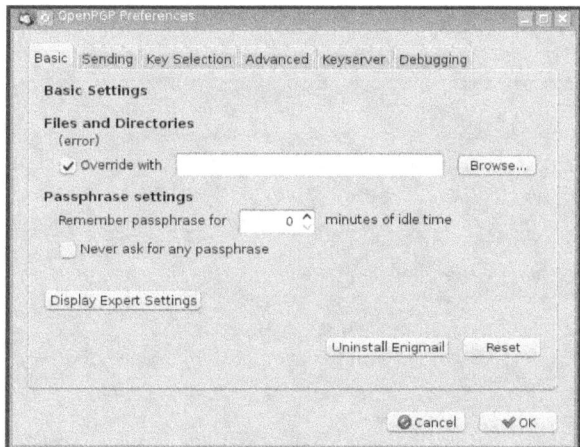

Here's the resulting file selection window, titled "Locate GnuPG program". You can see here where I found it, in /bin.

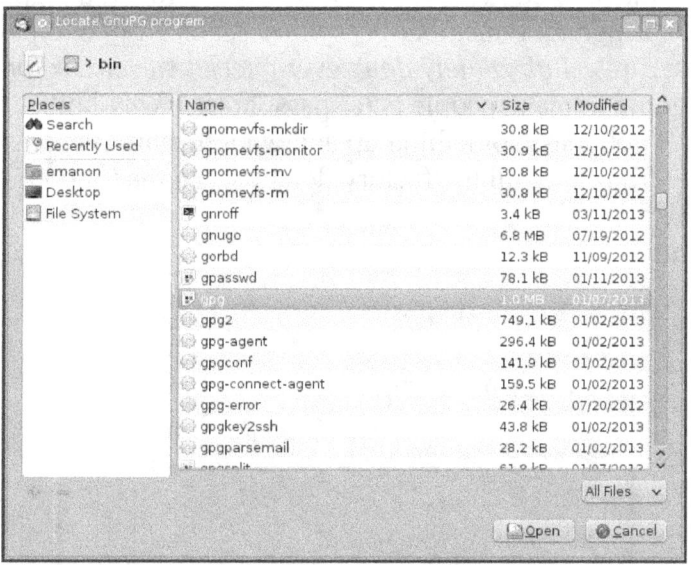

Clicking "Open" completed this part of the setup. Now, since our next task is to check the configuration of Enigmail, we want to go into "Expert Mode". Click "Display Expert Settings" to enable all of the detailed tabs Enigmail offers. There are some useful things you can set here, so we'll spend a few minutes setting them up before we move on to the next topic. Just set up your tabs the way I've set up mine; I'll explain all the settings underneath an image of each tab. If you want to do something differently, feel free; I'm just offering suggestions here.

First, the Basic tab:

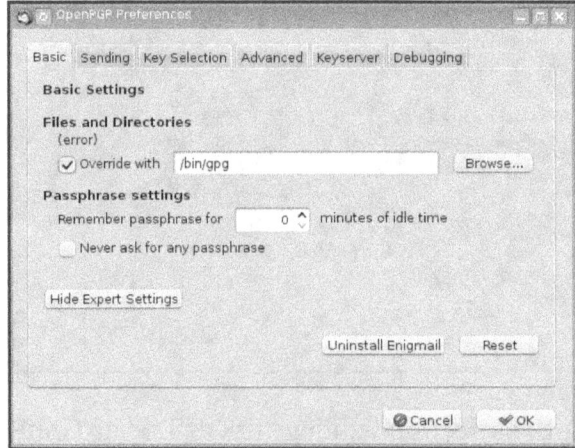

There's nothing much to do here, since we've already found the gpg binary (it was in "/bin/gpg"). I never let Enigmail remember passphrases, since I like to have to enter them every time (it's more secure). *I absolutely don't ever check "Never ask for any passphrase"* because if you're not going to make people enter passphrases, why bother encrypting in the first place? Note that if you mess something up and want to start over fresh, you can click "Reset" and Enigmail will restore all the factory defaults. So that's about it for the Basic tab.

The Sending tab:

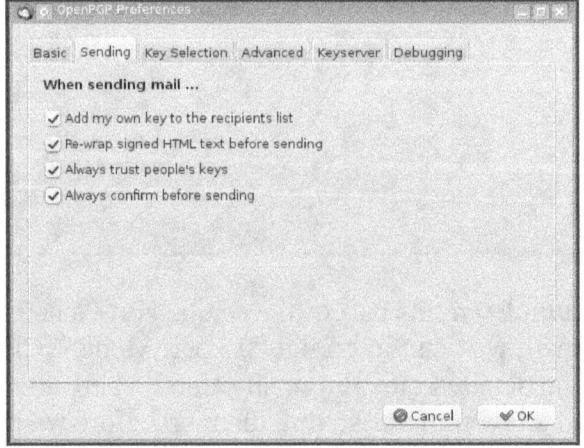

Ok, here, I checked everything. Adding my own key to the recipient's list allows me to read the messages I encrypt for other people. If you don't need that, you can uncheck it, but then you can't go back and see what you said. Re-wrapping signed HTML seems to make sure that if you've signed an HTML message, the signature doesn't get screwed up by the HTML. Always confirm before sending is just a safety net, letting me think a little longer before sending a message. Finally, there's "Always trust people's keys". That deserves some explanation.

You'll notice that I've checked the setting "Always trust other people's keys". When I was working on the Windows edition of this book, this setting caused me loads of trouble, preventing me from encrypting things using my gmail public key. It was driving me completely bonkers; I'd start an email to my gmail address, search the keyserver for the public key I'd just uploaded, and find out that Enigmail simply refused to let me encrypt with that key! As it turned out, this was how Enigmail was supposed to work, because it didn't *trust* that key. And here we need to talk about "Web of Trust".

The "Web of Trust" is a concept that was invented to help people determine if someone's encryption keys are authentic. The idea is that people who have downloaded someone else's key can sign it themselves, attaching a level of trust to the key. If a few different people have all decided that they trust a key, then that key is probably trustworthy, at least in theory. This sounds absolutely brilliant to socially active academics, who have lots of encryption-using academic friends and eager to please grad students, all willing to vouch for them. What could possibly go wrong?

The problem with this whole concept is, when you're a crazy hermit like me, and you have no friends (or at least, no friends who use encryption) the heroic-sounding Web of Trust totally marginalizes you. Because nobody has signed your key, by default nobody can use your key to send you anything; by default, Enigmail and GnuPG *don't trust your key*. Thus, the Web of Trust is the enemy of loners and other associated weirdos, a force locking us right OUT, further alienating and marginalizing us. It's all just bricks in the wall, to paraphrase one of the motivational hymns of my youth.

The answer to this problem is to check the item "Always trust other people's keys". This way, even if someone is an antisocial, misanthropic weirdo like me, you can find our public keys and encrypt stuff to send to us. If you're worried about encrypting something with the wrong key, all you have to do is coordinate with us in advance, and trade keys (on thumbdrives, say, or via email). Honestly, this is a better approach than using a keyserver anyway. Sure, you can search by email, but it's still easy to pick the wrong key, or an old key, or end up with a key whose passphrase the guy's' forgotten (I have at least two of those). Coordinate key exchanges in person or by email, and agree in advance on some ground rules.

By the way, *you shouldn't EVER send unsolicited, encrypted email to anybody*, unless you're trying to give them a heart attack. I delete stuff like that without opening it, because anything could be in there. Anything! Viruses, spam, etc... It's too risky. So, you know, if you're going to send something encrypted to somebody, you should probably give them a heads up first, and let them know what it is so they know it's safe to open. Just saying.

Let us proceed to the next tab.

The Key Selection Tab:

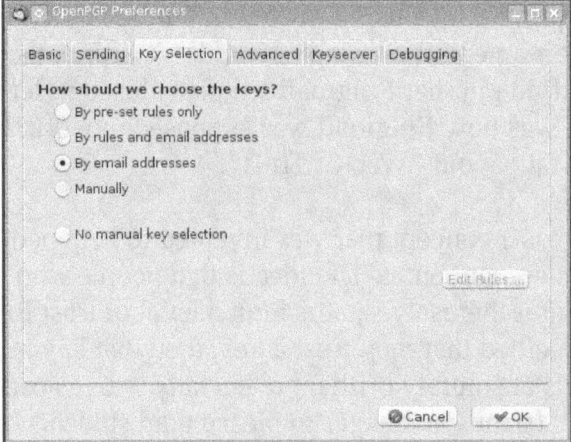

Here, all I did was choose to pick keys by email address. Keys are identified by email address, and it's more specific than the target's name. I think this is the easiest way to go.

The Advanced Tab:

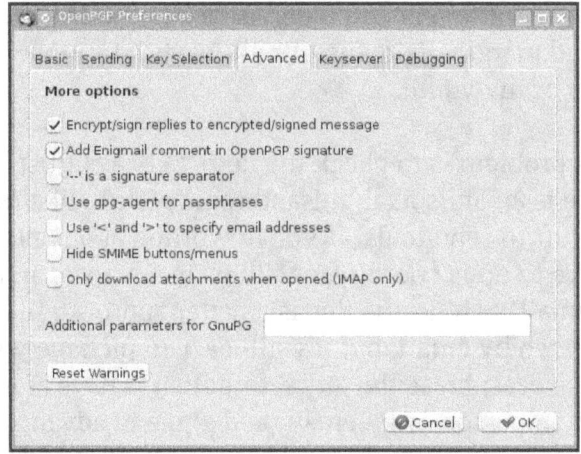

Here I was only interested in two things. First, if someone encrypts and/or signs something to send to me, I figure the least I can do is return the favor, so I checked the first option. Second, I chose to add Enigmail comments in OpenPGP signatures (why not give credit where credit is due?). The rest I left blank.

The next tab is the "Keyserver" tab, and even though I think it's better to exchange keys in person, I also think it's nice to have access to a keyserver. So the next tab will let us configure our preferred keyservers, which is a convenience worth setting up.

Protecting Your Privacy and Anonymity Online — Gnu/Linux Edition

The Keyserver tab:

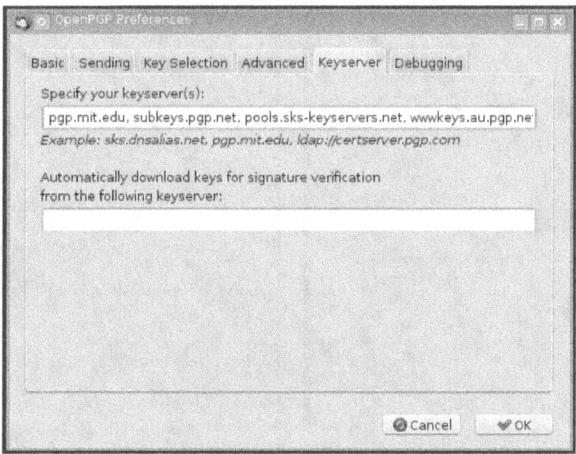

On the "Keyserver" tab, we've got a time-saver. We can enter in a list of keyservers (so when we search for a public key, we can choose a keyserver from a drop-down instead of having to manually enter it every single time). Also, we can set up a keyserver for automatically verifying signatures. I'm using "pgp.mit.edu" for my main keyserver, and "subkeys.pgp.net", "pools.sks-keyservers.net", and "wwwkeys.au.pgp.net" as my backup ones. This is a pretty good setup.

I didn't bother with the "Debugging" tab, so there's nothing to worry about there. Click "OK" to wrap up, and we can start configuring Enigmail for our actual email accounts.

Configuring EnigMail's OpenPGP Settings
For Your Email Accounts

Before we go any further, we have to set up our email account's OpenPGP settings. There are two ways to do this; there's a wizard, which is easy, and there's directly configuring the account, which is also easy (but not quite as easy).

Let's try the wizard first. To run the wizard, click the options button in the upper right hand corner of Thunderbird, then click "OpenPGP", then click "Setup Wizard", like in the next screenshot. By the way, you notice how many more options we have now? When we enabled the Expert Settings, we didn't just get the Enigmail preferences tabs, we also got all sorts of extra menu items, a great side effect.

Notice that I've taken two screenshots here. On the left, you can see the way the menu appears by default, with "Automatically Decrypt/Verify Messages" enabled. That's terrible! You want to be able to decide NOT to decrypt something, if you think it's fishy or you don't trust the sender. So, disable that setting, as I have in the screenshot on the right. It's SAFER.

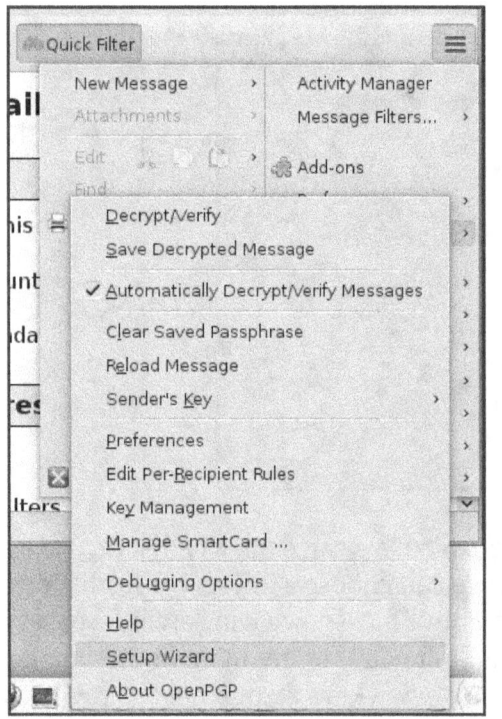 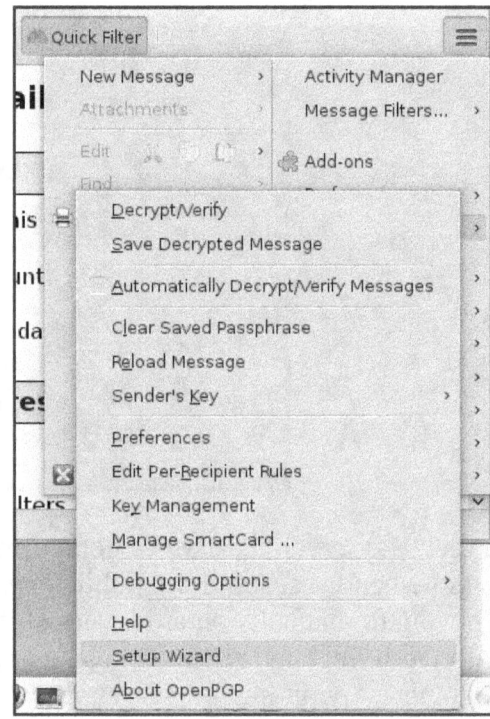

The wizard has seven steps; here they are, in order. You don't really have to change anything because the defaults are pretty good. Note that I've blurred out my own data, and made some minor changes out of personal preference. I'll mention what they were.

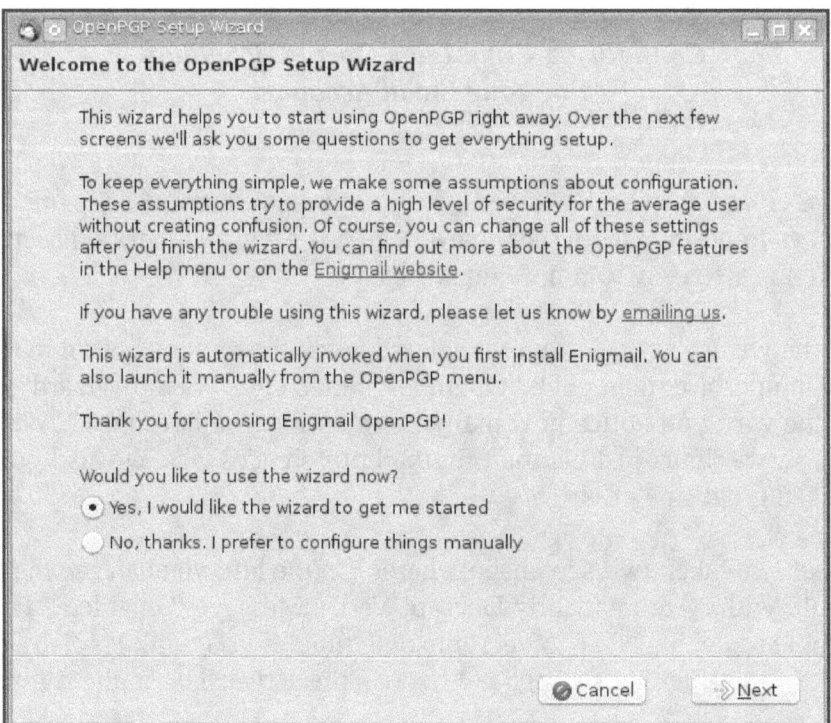

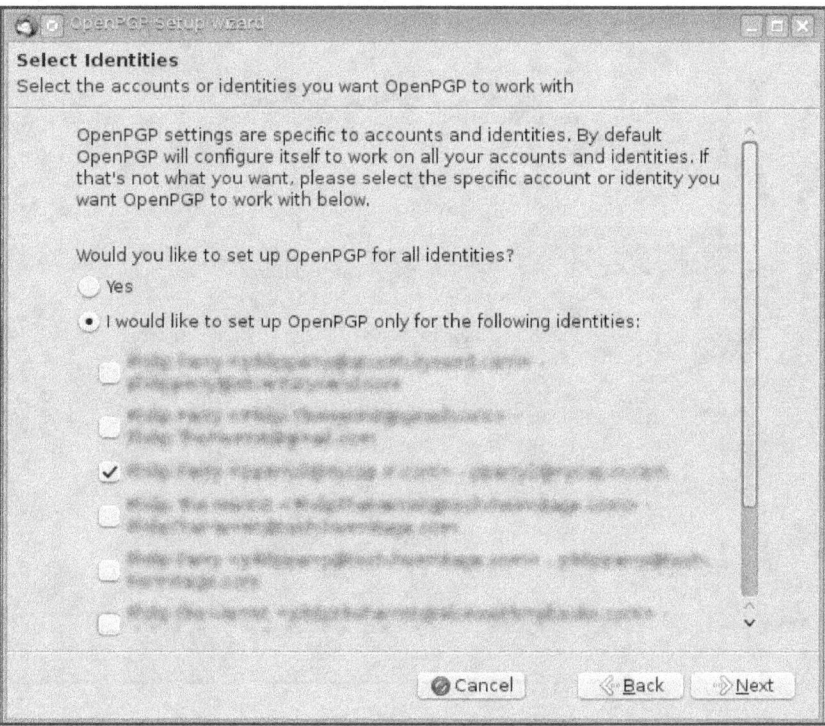

Above, I changed the default from "Yes" to selecting individual accounts. Below, I chose not to sign all my email, because I don't feel like doing that.

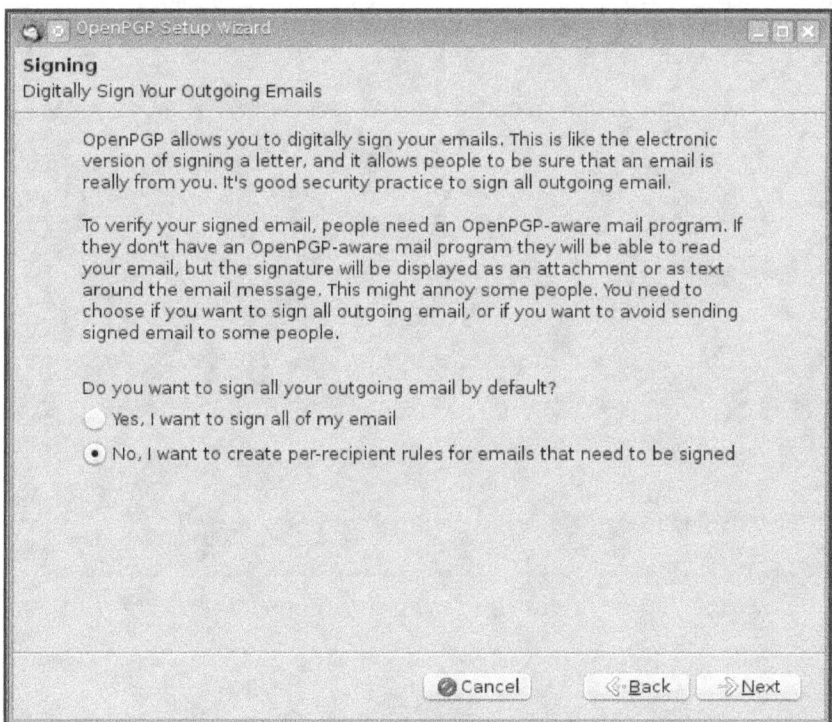

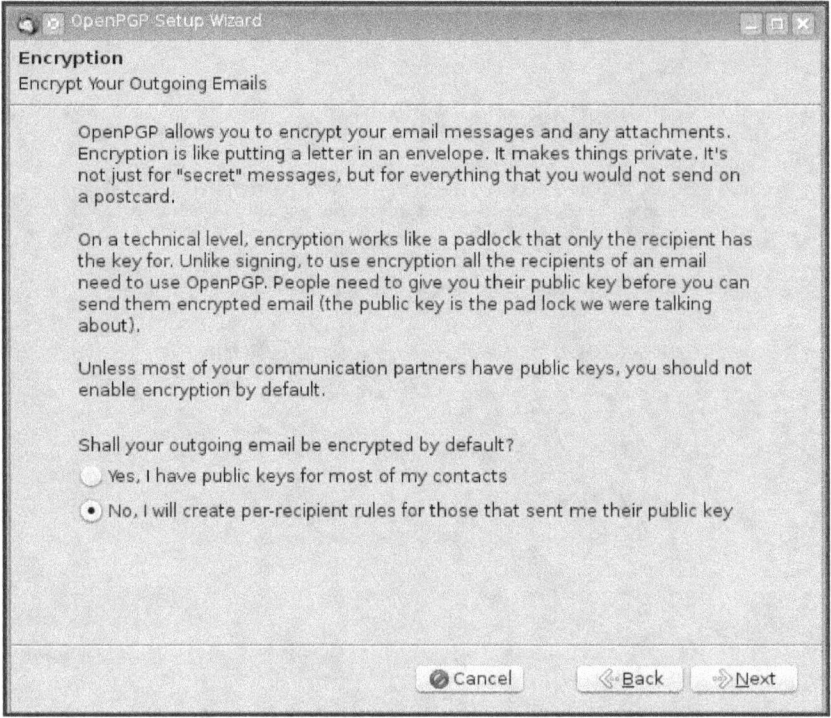

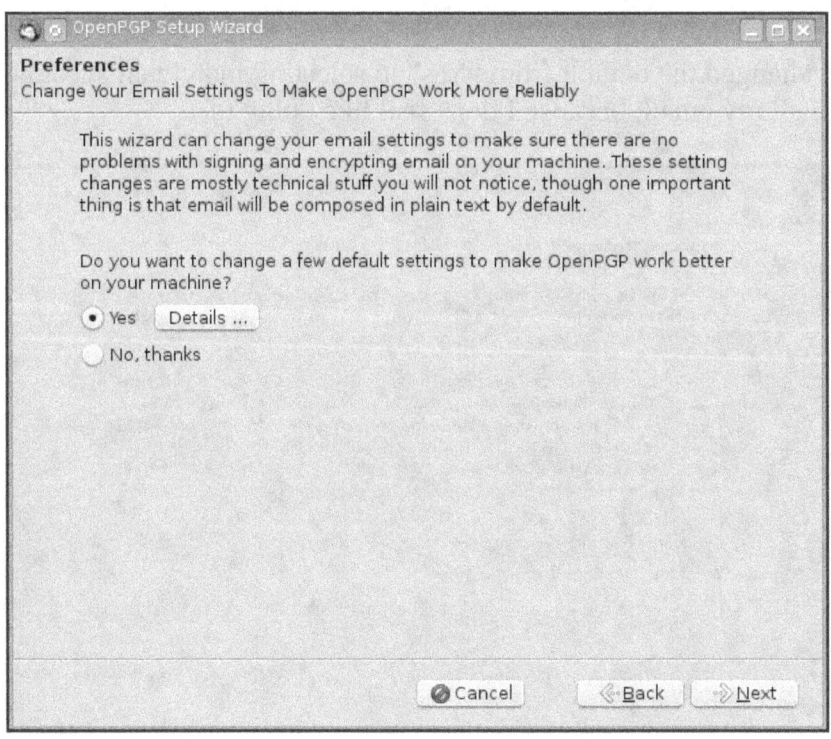

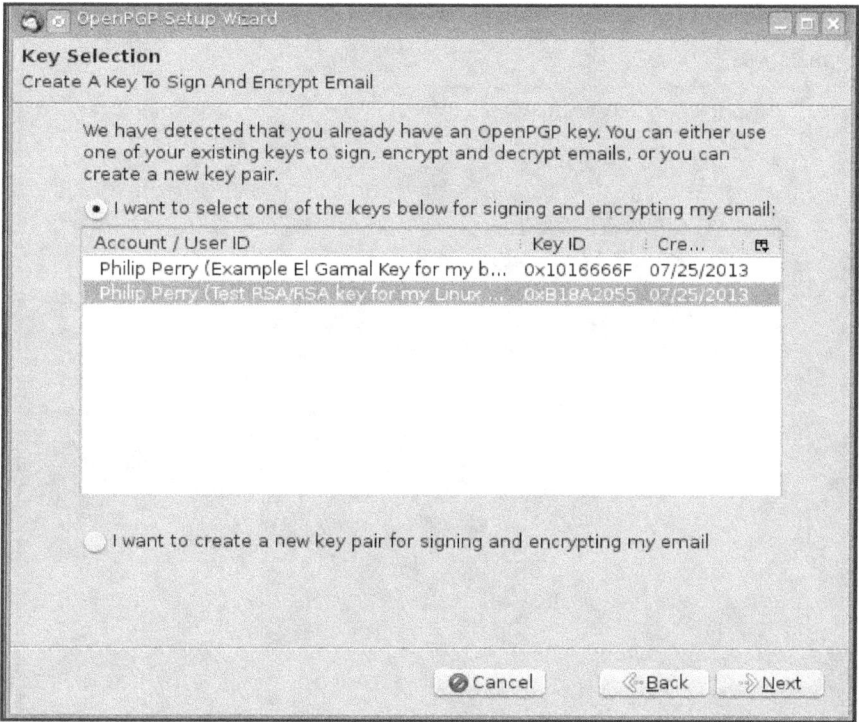

Here, I picked one of the keys I set up while working on the GnuPG chapter.

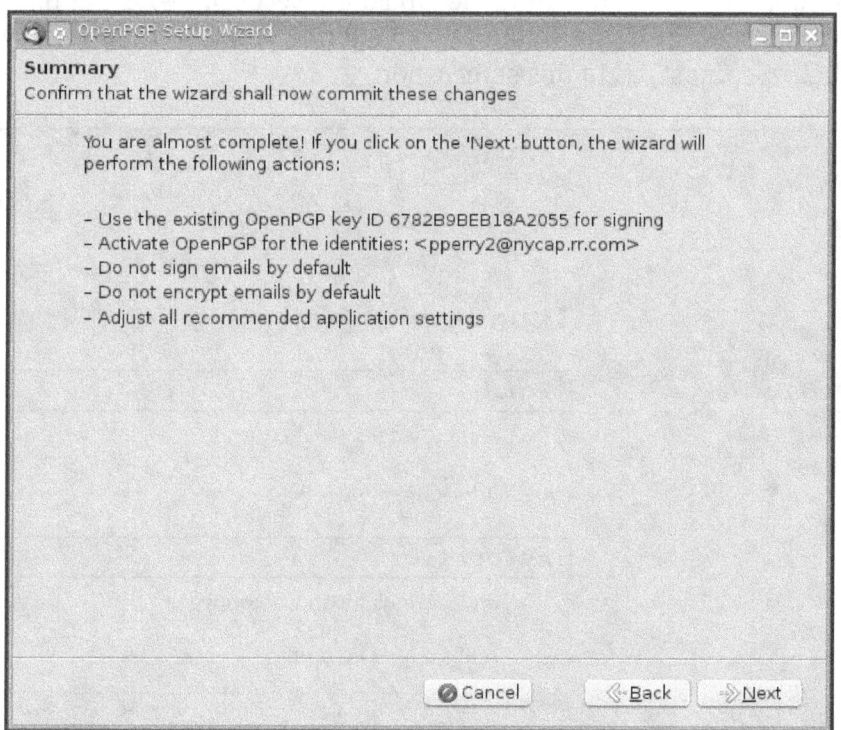

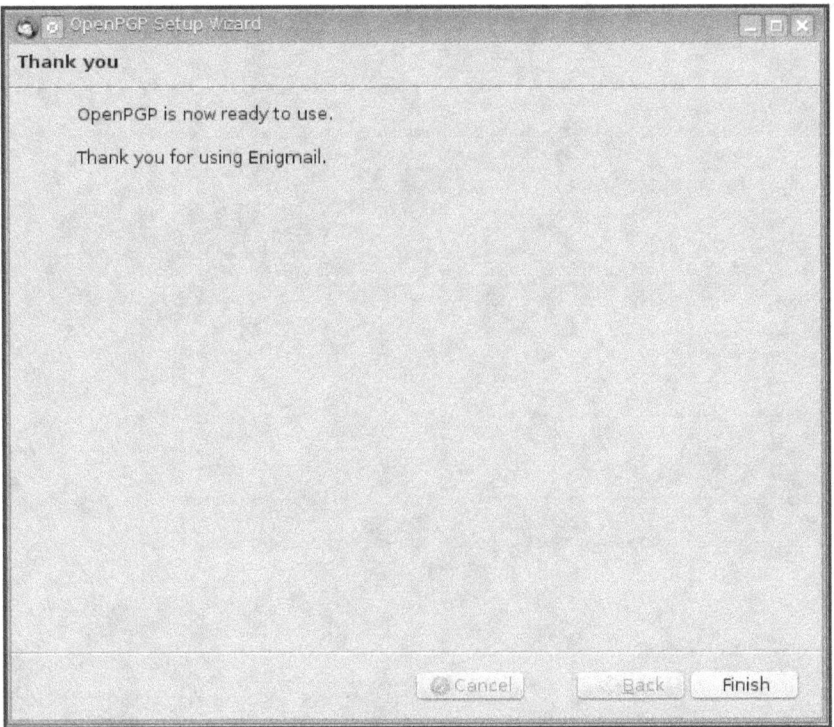

The wizard is pretty straightforward, but you can also configure your account by going directly to the account settings and editing the OpenPGP section. Note that this is also a good way to fine-tune your settings if you want to do so later. To do this, right-click your email account, then click "Settings", as in this screenshot:

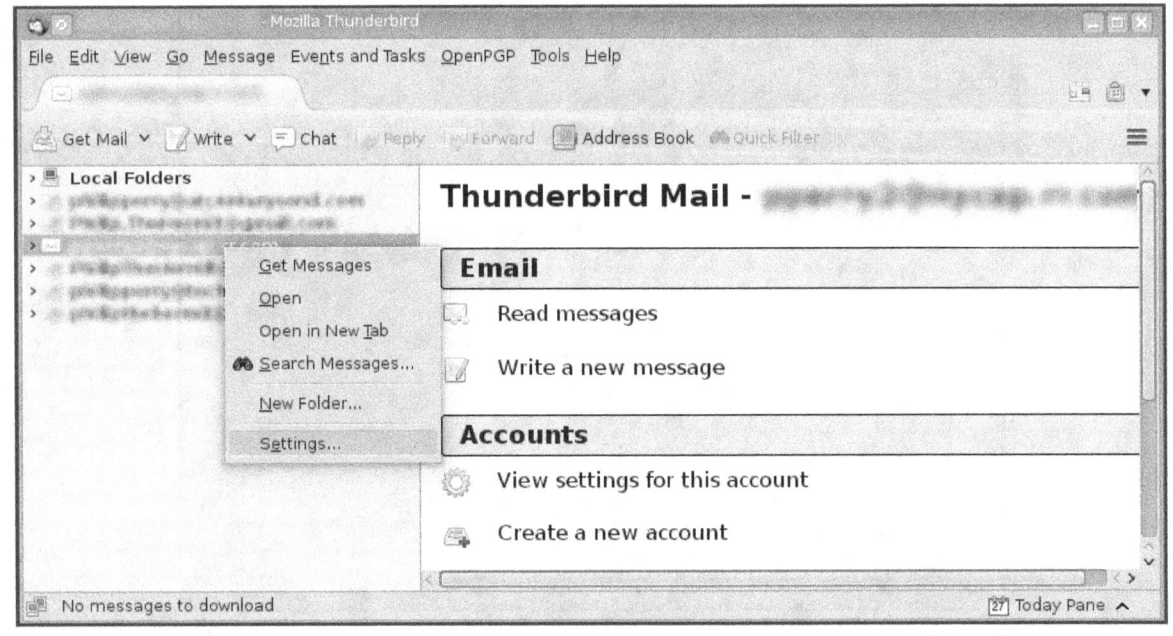

The settings window that pops up looks like the screenshot below. Click "OpenPGP Settings" as I have in the screenshot, which brings up the setup tool you see on the right side.

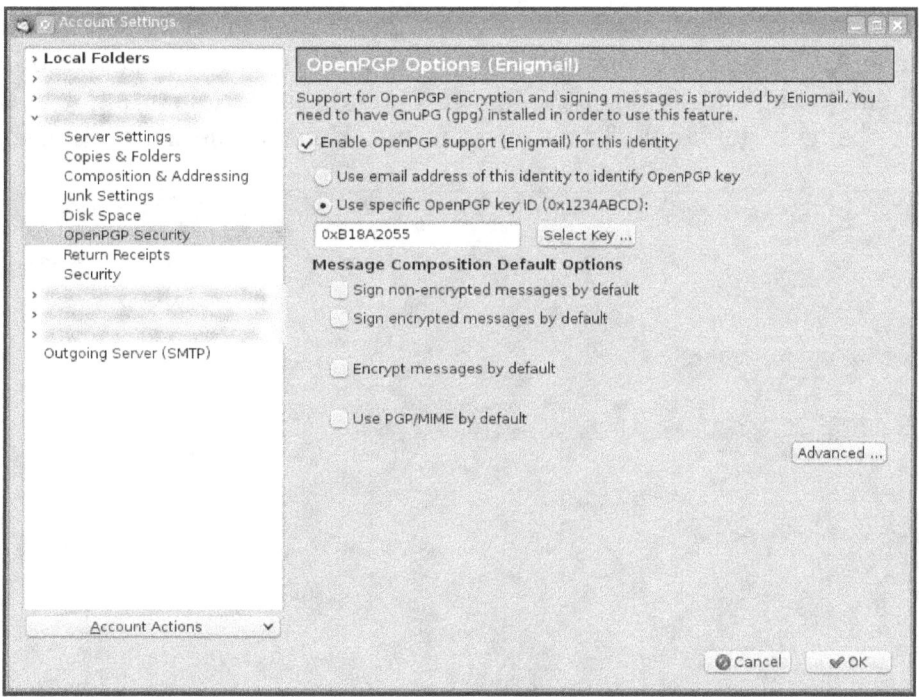

Here, I've enabled OpenPGP support for this email account, and I've chosen to use a specific OpenPGP key already stored in my GnuPG setup. I've accepted the other defaults, leaving the other options un-checked. Also, I blurred out my email addresses for privacy. Clicking the "Select Key" button brings up the window in the next screenshot, in which you can see two keys I set up back in the GnuPG chapter. Once you've set these items, click "OK" and you're done; Thunderbird will now use your GnuPG setup with your email account.

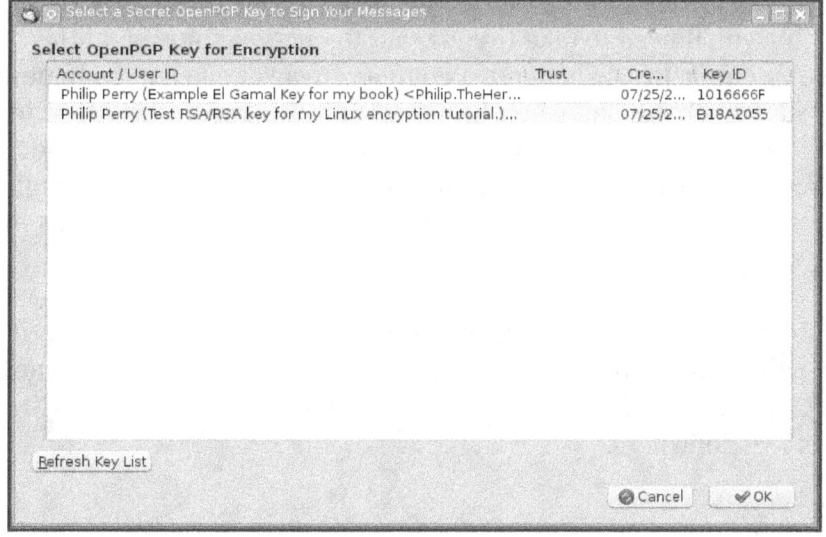

Note that the secret key you choose will be used to decrypt messages being sent to you encrypted with your public key, as well as to sign encrypted messages you're sending out.

While you're in the settings for this account, there's another thing you should do. Click "Composition & Addressing" and disable HTML-formatted email. Apparently, this can interfere with encrypting and signing messages (I found this out while trying to encrypt a message, so it's better to get it out of the way up front). Here are the settings I used:

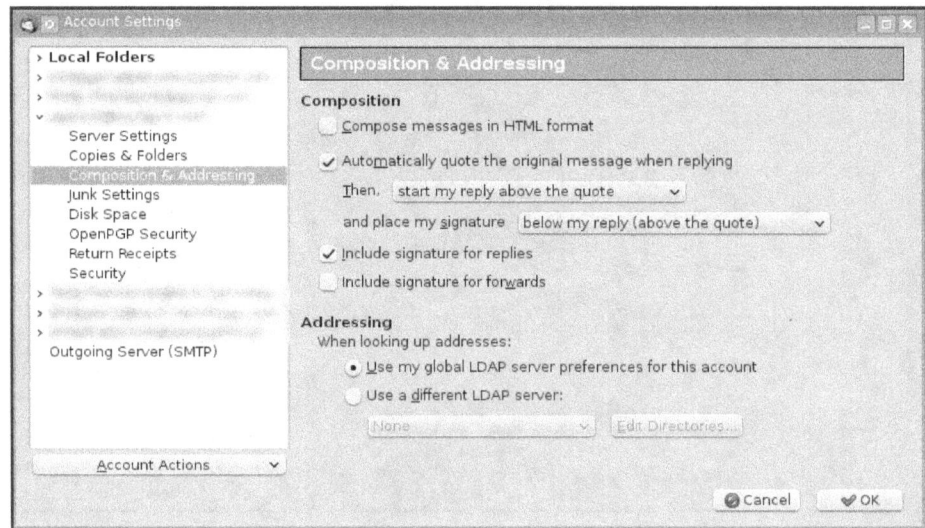

So far, everything's been pretty straightforward. Now we'd like to actually start sending encrypted email to people.

Encrypting Email With Enigmail

The first step you'll need to take if you want to encrypt some email for someone is to acquire that person's public key. There are a couple of ways you can go about this. The first way is to simply start an email, and when Enigmail pops up a window informing you that you don't have a public key for that person, you search for it on the key server and import it. Note that this will import the key into GnuPG for you, not just Enigmail. So, let's give this a try, since it'll let us work through the process of encrypting an email and it lets us hit two birds with one stone.

First, on the Thunderbird main screen, click the "Write" item in the toolbar at the top of the screen. This will open a composition window, which you can see on the next page. Note that we're not encrypting by default, so we have to deliberately select that. Click "OpenPGP", then "Encrypt" as I've done here.

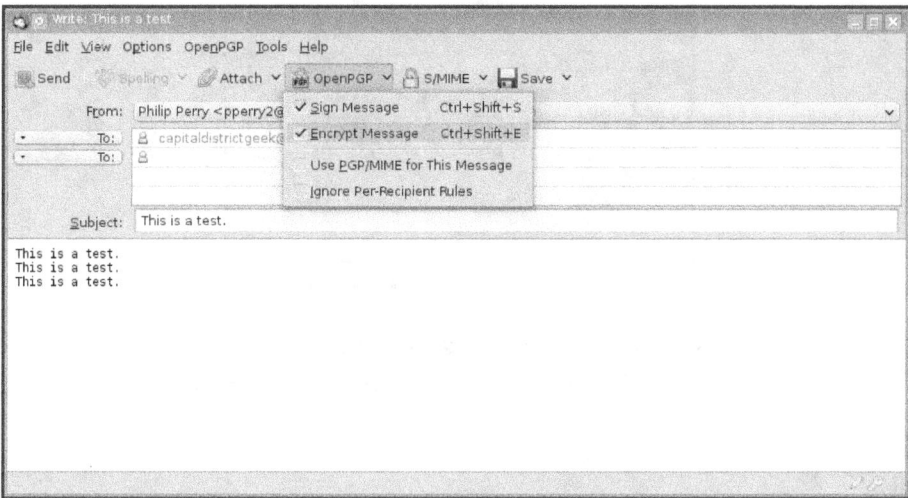

When you click "Send", Enigmail will figure out that you don't have a public key that's associated with the target email address, so it'll pop up the window in the next screenshot to ask you to help it find one:

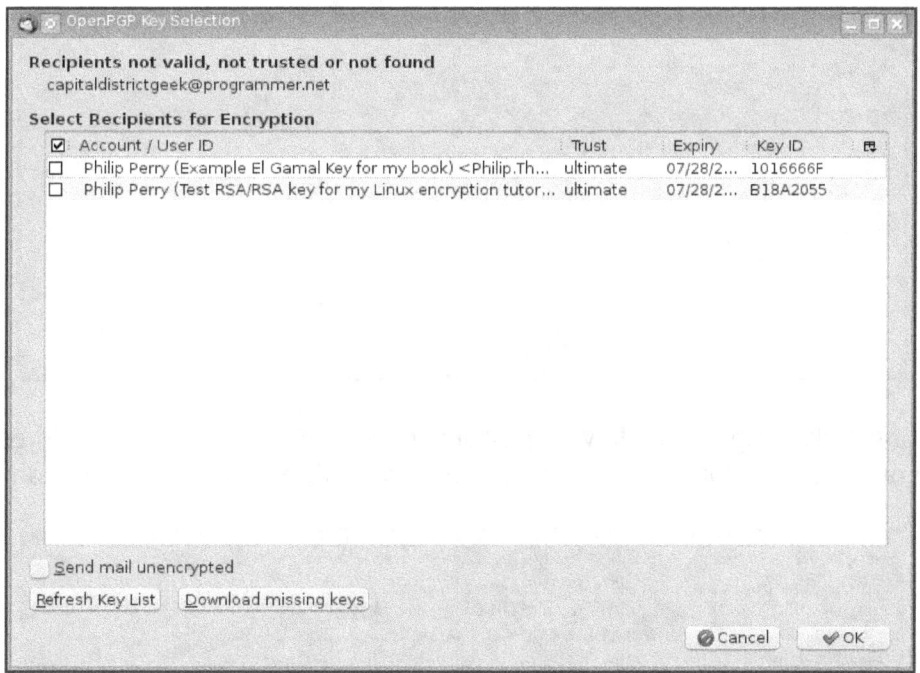

Click the "Download missing keys" button to look up the email address on one of the keyservers we configured a short while ago. You should see the following window pop up, allowing you to choose which keyserver you search for the email address' public keys. Since we set up the keyserver list earlier, it's pre-populated for us:

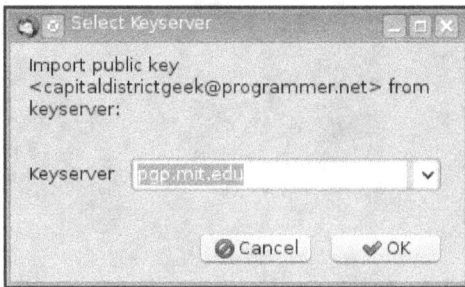

Clicking "OK" brings up any results Enigmail finds, such as the one you see in the next screenshot. Try to choose the most recent key in the list, since it's probably the most up to date.

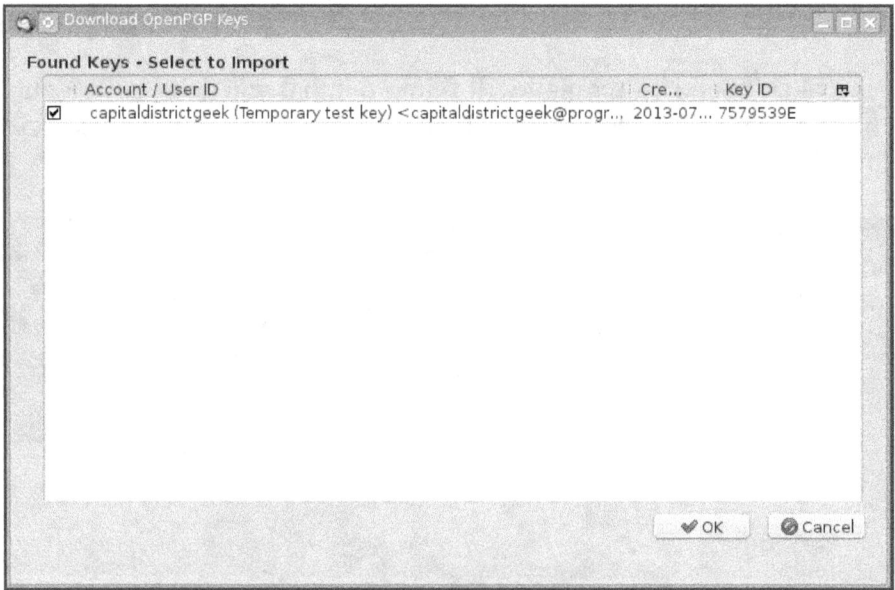

Clicking "OK" imports the key and associates it with the target email address you're encrypting a message for. Once it's imported, Enigmail will pop up a confirmation message:

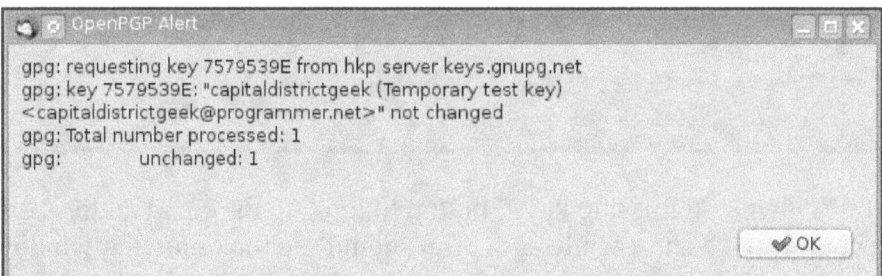

When you click "OK", you'll be taken back to the original window which asked you to choose an encryption key to use with this email address. You can see it in the next screenshot. Select the new one, then click "OK".

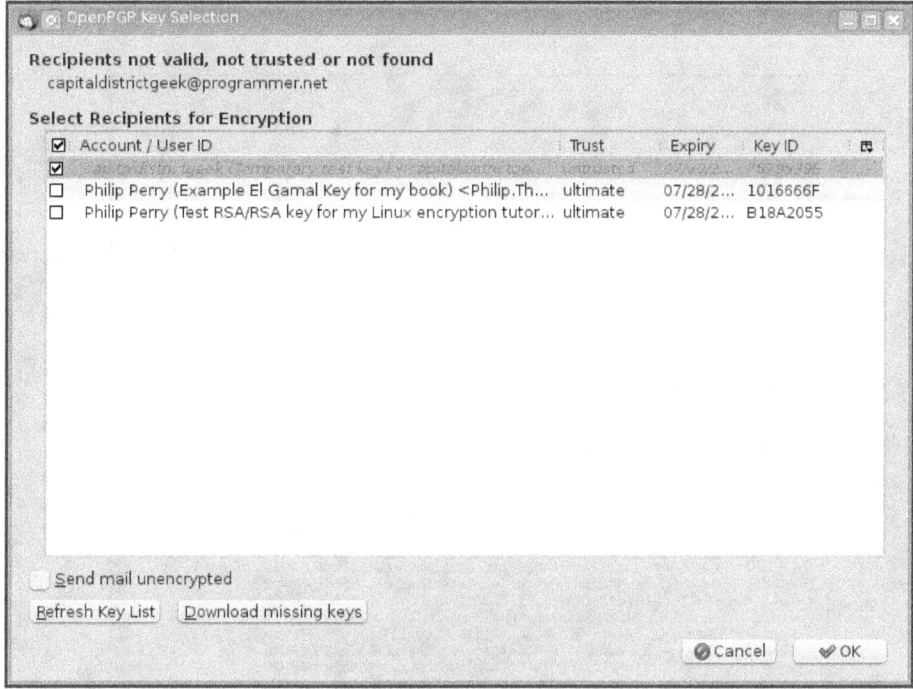

Now Enigmail is ready to encrypt our email and send it off, but first (because I chose to sign it) we have to give our pass phrase. This is the phrase for our secret key, which is used to sign documents.

After you click "OK", Enigmail encrypts and sends the email. This goes by so quickly, it's almost impossible to capture a screenshot, but it's not very eventful anyway. The point is, the email has been encrypted using the recipient's public key, and signed with your private key. A new confirmation comes up, because I asked for confirmation in one of the settings, although right now I don't remember where (hmm). Clicking "Send Message" sends the message on its merry way.

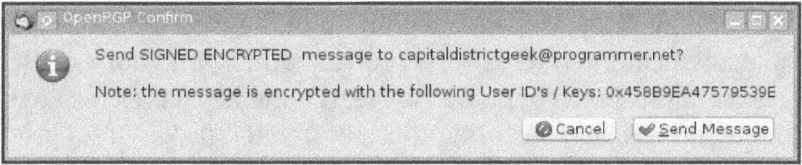

Now let's look at it in the "sent" folder, so we can see what it looks like before it's decrypted.

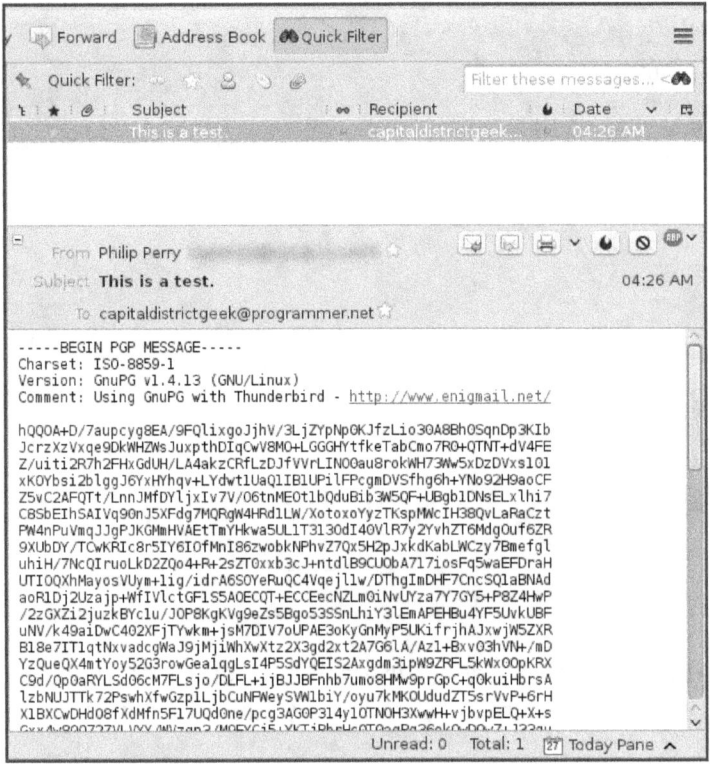

As you can see, the email is encrypted, and we can't look at it without A) having the secret key that goes with the email address it was sent to, and B) entering the pass phrase.

So that's how to send someone an encrypted email, picking up their public encryption key in the process. This is the easiest way to encrypt email for people, and generally how you should go about it (although, again, I think it's more reliable to trade keys in person). If you want to import a bunch of keys in advance, because you know you'll be communicating with some group of people and you don't want to have to import their keys while you send each email, you can do that through Enigmail's key management tool. We'll look at this next.

Key Management With Enigmail

First, start up Enigmail's key management tool. Click Thunderbird's options button, then OpenPGP. Clicking the "Key Management" item in the OpenPGP drop-down menu brings up the key management interface. Here you can work with your GnuPG keychain, you can import new keys from the keyserver, you can search the keyserver for keys relating to a specific name or email address, and perform other key-related tasks. It's a pretty good tool overall, and you'll get a lot of use out of it. The main key management window appears in the next screenshot.

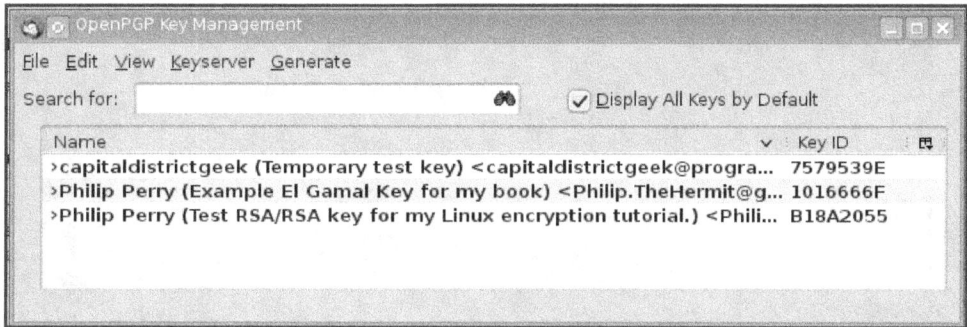

Here, you can see three keys: two from the GnuPG chapter, and one I created to create email screenshots a short while ago. Note that I've checked "Display All Keys by Default"; this shows you all your keys, not just the ones that match search terms you've entered in the box to the left. I generally like to leave this checked, so I don't have to hunt for things. I'm going to right-click on the first key and delete it so we can search the keyserver for it, so you can see how to do that. To search the keyserver, click "Keyserver", then "Search for Keys", as in the next screenshot.

The search interface that comes up looks like this (I'm searching by email address):

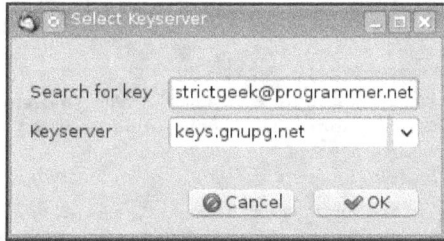

Entering an email address or name in the search box, then clicking "OK" gives you a window containing search results, as in the next screenshot. Generally you should look for the most recent one, I think; but make sure it's the public key of the person you actually want to get ahold of.

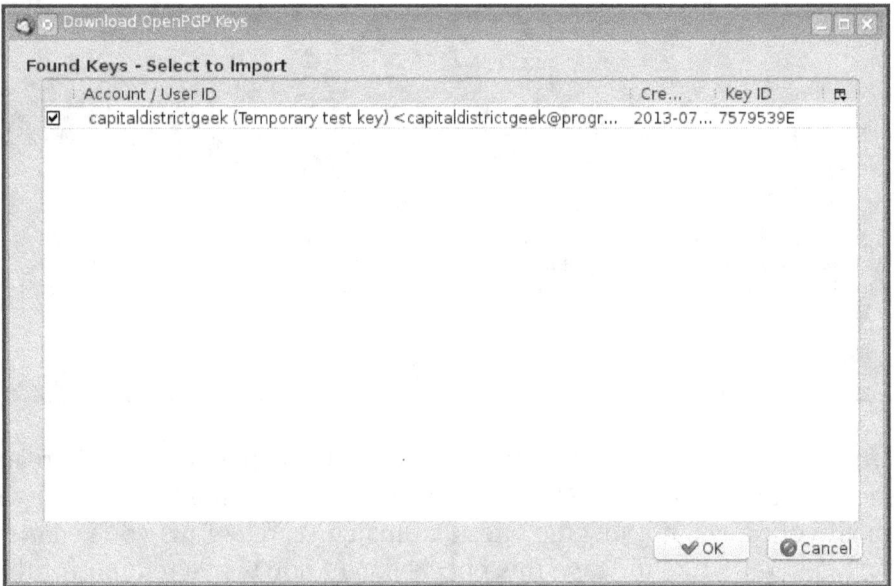

As before, when we click "OK" we get a confirmation popup:

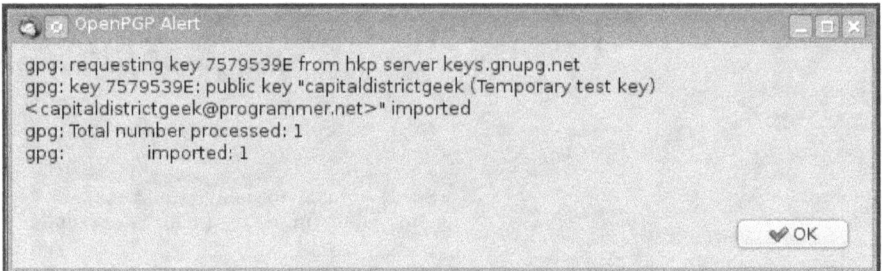

And when we click "OK" again, we see that the key has been acquired.

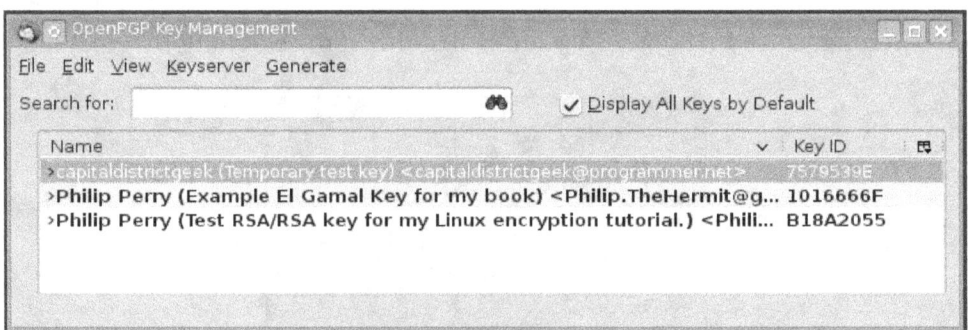

So, that's the important part of the key management tool -- finding and acquiring the keys of people you wish to communicate with. Of course, there's a lot more to Enigmail, and Enigmail has a pretty good manual if you want to learn about it. You can find it here:

http://www.enigmail.net/home/index.php

Before we wrap up this chapter, let's look at one more thing: decrypting an email.

Remember how we said we don't want to automatically decrypt mail, because someone nefarious could send us something terrible? Well, if we decide an email is safe to open, we can decrypt it with the "Decrypt" button on the Thunderbird toolbar. Let's go through that process next.

Decrypting an Encrypted Message You've Received

This is so easy it almost doesn't warrant its own section. For the sake of this example, I've encrypted a message to myself. You can see it in my Inbox, in the following screenshot. On Gnu/Linux, you have to click the "OpenPGP" menu, then "Decrypt/Verify", as in the following screenshot.

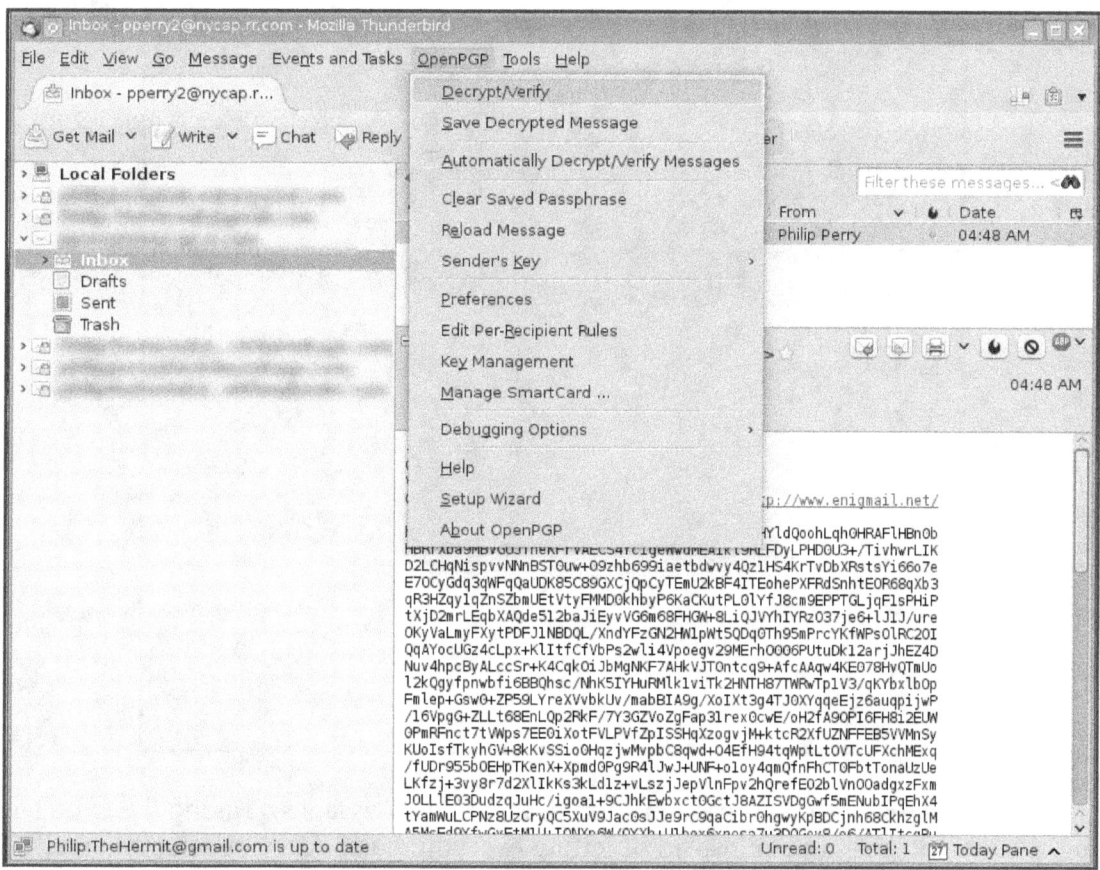

Clicking the "Decrypt/Verify" menu item results in the following pop-up window:

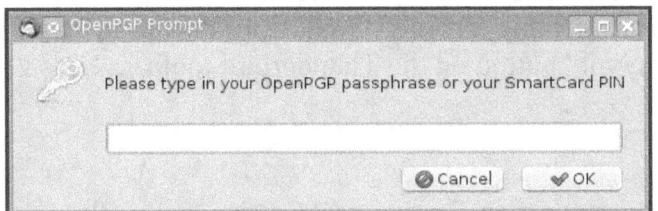

And, after correctly entering my encryption pass-phrase and clicking "OK", I get the decrypted, verified message you can see in the next screenshot (sorry I keep blurring out my email addresses, but a guy's got to be careful about such things):

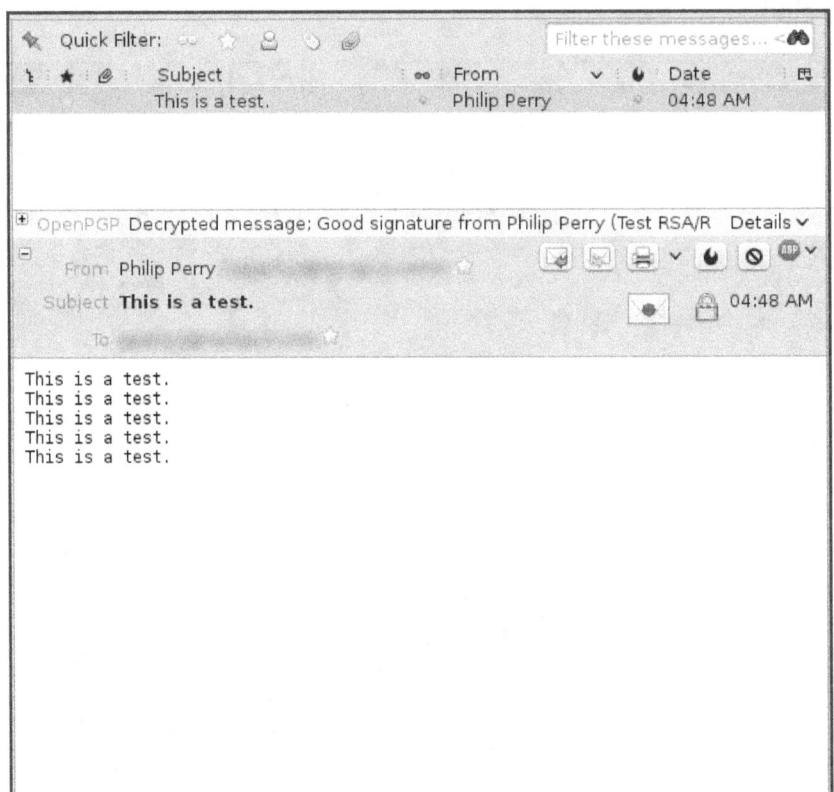

As you can see, it's pretty easy to decrypt incoming messages. Taking the extra step of clicking a "Decrypt" menu item instead of letting everything get decrypted automatically doesn't really inconvenience us at all, and it offers us valuable benefits. We don't have to worry about unscrupulous Feds sending us weird stuff to entrap us, and we don't have to worry about trojans and viruses from weirdos we've never met, and best of all we don't have to worry about someone reading our email when we've stepped away from our desk.

That about wraps it up for email encryption; now let's look at text messaging.

Chapter 5:

Instant Messaging

Now that we've looked at browsing the web anonymously, acquiring anonymous email and forum accounts, encrypting our files to protect them, and encrypting our email to prevent eavesdropping, it's time to address instant messaging. Since we can do everything else privately and anonymously, we should be able to do this privately and anonymously as well.

First, some good news. Where in my other books, I generally "get the unpleasantries out of the way" at this point, and warn you about commonly available tools which don't protect your anonymity and security, here we're using Gnu/Linux, and the standard Gnu/Linux tools for instant messaging are already secure and very anonymity friendly. So your life has once again been made a lot easier by the open source community, and that is a beautiful thing.

While we're on this topic, I'd like to point something out that I think is important. Whenever you're doing instant messaging, depending on the protocol you're using your conversation is either going peer-to-peer (i.e. directly between your PC and your friend's) or it's going through some company's servers. If you're chatting via a website which offers IM services, your conversation is going through their servers and can be monitored. If you're going directly peer-to-peer, unless your conversation is encrypted it can be monitored. So, pay attention to the protocol you're using and use Tor and/or encryption appropriately. A nice thing about the Gnu/Linux tools is that they don't care what protocol you're using (ICQ, IRC, AOL IM, etc) they allow you to use Tor and encryption independently. So that's pretty cool.

I've identified three tools which I'm sure you'll be interested in. For Tor-based anonymous chats over your Tor Browser, there's Cryptocat, a plugin available for Mozilla Firefox (and therefore, the Tor Browser). Cryptocat is magnificent, and the U.S. government dislikes its creator (they famously hassled him about Cryptocat during a border crossing), which for me is a terrific endorsement. Next, there's Off the Record, a tool which supports encrypted text messaging. Off the Record creates new encryption keys on the fly for each instant message you send, giving you "perfect forward secrecy". Finally, Pidgin is an instant messaging tool which supports virtually all the currently used chat protocols, supports Off the Record encryption via a plugin, and can work with Tor. Put these tools together and you've got everything you need. Let's get cracking.

Cryptocat and the Tor Browser for Anonymous, Encrypted Chat

Acquiring Cryptocat is a piece of cake. Just fire up Tor, and within the Tor Browser, go to the Mozilla Firefox "Add-ons" page. You can find the Add-ons site by clicking the "tools" menu, then clicking "Add-ons" as in the following screenshot:

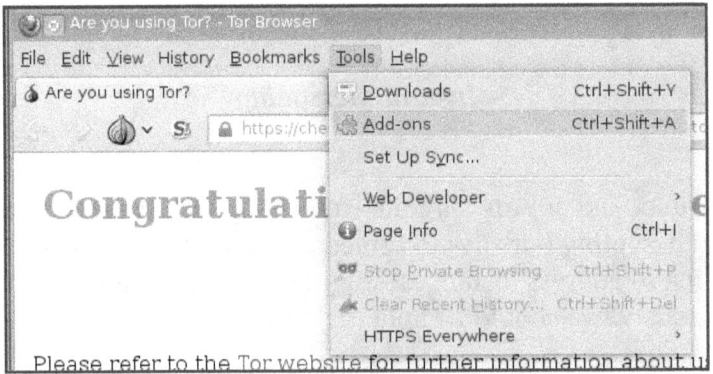

Clicking the "Add-ons" link takes you to the Firefox Add-ons site, where you can search for Cryptocat, as you can see in the following image. Here, I've put highlighted the Cryptocat plugin. Note that there are a lot of related plugins available. Be careful what you acquire; pick up the wrong tool, and you might compromise your privacy and anonymity. Remember, the government does not like Cryptocat.

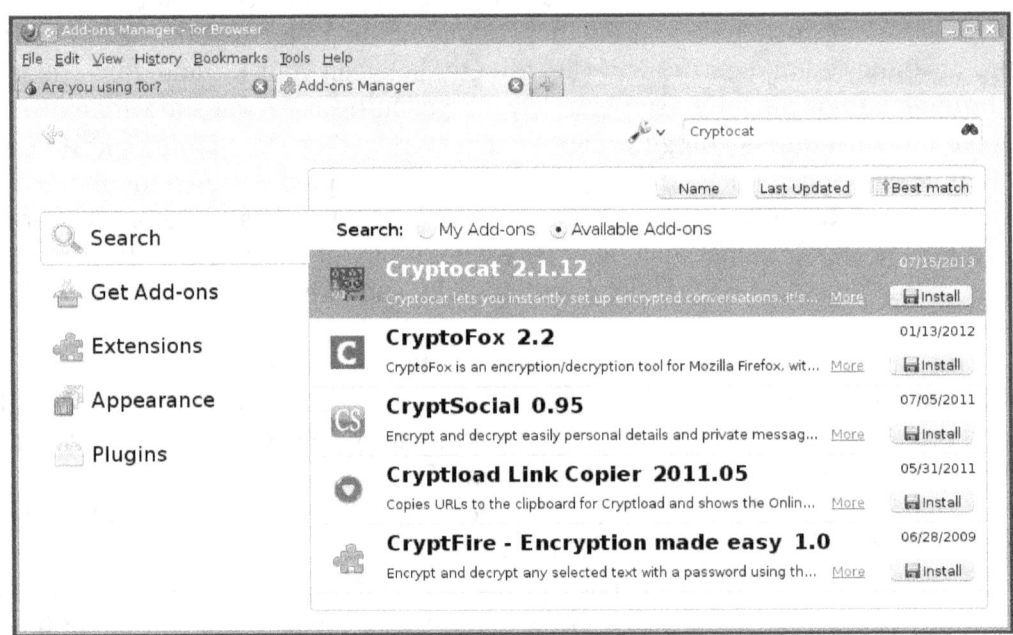

Before you install Cryptocat, please click the "more" link next to the install button and read what the developer has to say. It's very interesting. When you're done, go ahead and click "Install". You'll see a download progress bar, then the following confirmation; click "Restart now" to complete the installation.

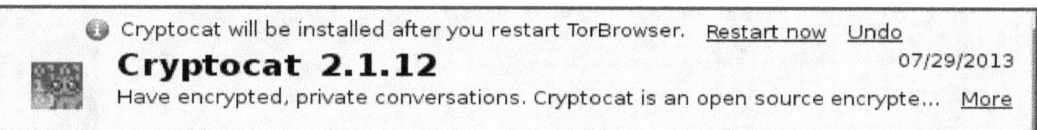

Once the Tor Browser restarts, you'll see Cryptocat in the upper right hand corner of your browser window, to the right of the home button, as in the next image. Here, my mouse pointer isn't visible in the screenshot, but you can see the Cryptocat button is highlighted and the tooltip is floating just under it. Click the Cryptocat button to open up Cryptocat.

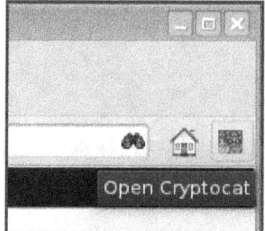

Here's what Cryptocat looks like when you run it. Note that you can enter a name for a conversation you want to create or join, and give yourself an anonymous nickname for use during the conversation. You can just go straight to the "lobby" if you just want to chat with whoever's around, as well. Here, I've called myself "ILikeMyPrivacy" and I've used a conversation name "PrivacyTest1". Of course, in practice you're might want to use something like the anonymous email address you use with the person you'll be talking with. You can use that anonymous email account (while using Tor!) to give your friend instructions on how to set up Cryptocat and let him know what conversation name you're choosing, too.

Protecting Your Privacy and Anonymity Online — Gnu/Linux Edition

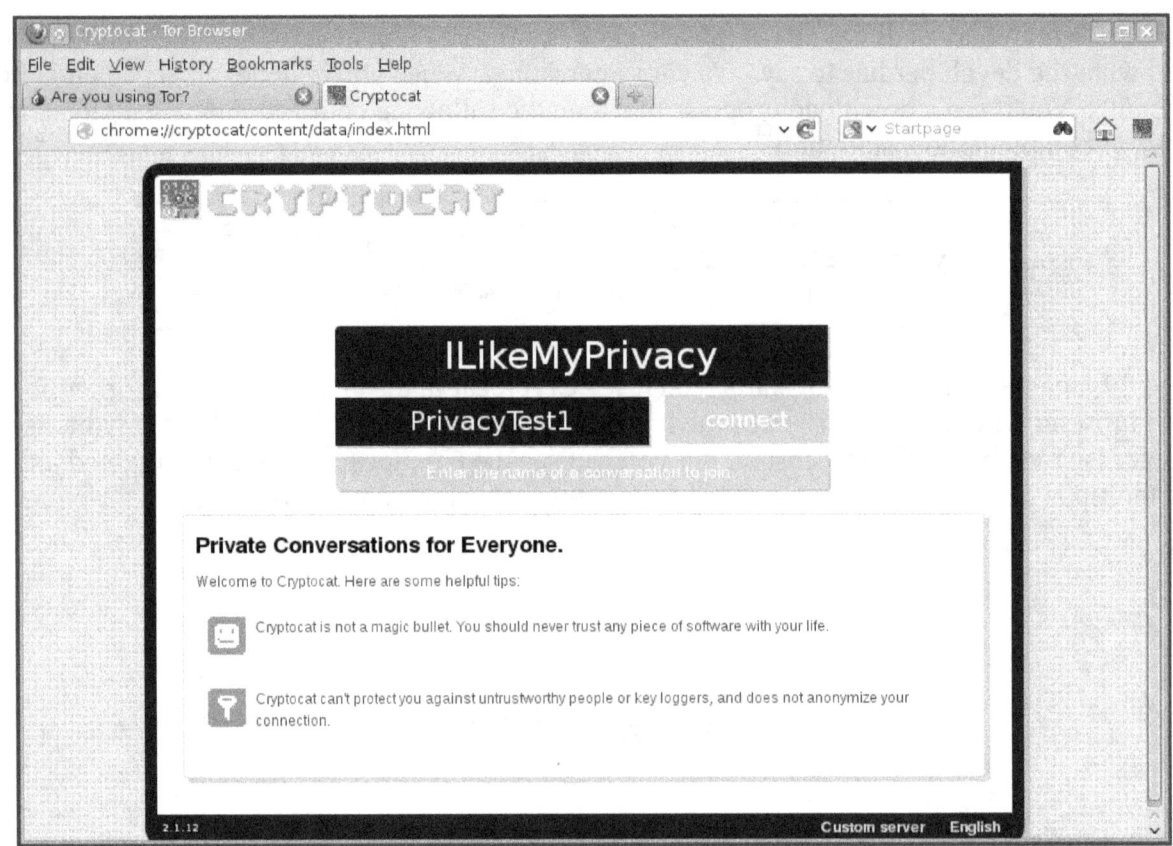

Note the two tips: interestingly, the second tip has been partially dealt with by connecting to Cryptocat over Tor, which *does* anonymize your connection. *However, their other points are important.* You have to be able to trust the person you're chatting with not to spill the beans, and you have to make sure your computer hasn't been compromised because a keylogger (which governments *love* to use) can still capture everything you say.

Keyloggers come in two forms. A software keylogger is usually packed on a thumbdrive, and someone sneaks into your house and installs it on your PC when you're not around. Alternately, if they can trick you into opening an email attachment, they might try that too (this is why you don't click on things in email). A hardware keylogger is usually a little plug that goes between your keyboard and your PC, or gets tucked inside your laptop somewhere. Then, everything you type gets stored on the keylogger, and it either uploads your activity from time to time or someone comes around and physically picks it up. Governments legally use them, private investigators *illegally* use them, and stupid people sometimes buy them in "Spy Stores" to snoop on their spouses and wreck their marriages. They're evil little things, and I hate them. As long as we're on the topic, I might as well give you an idea of what to do about them.

You can make it really, really hard to install a software keylogger on your system. First, set a BIOS password, so they can't log in without getting past that (this requires them to open up the PC and try to reset the BIOS, something you'll notice when you get back because the BIOS password will be gone). Next, make sure you use full-disk encryption as I discussed in the GnuPG chapter. Encrypting the hard disk makes it impossible to boot your system without knowing the passphrase, and this prevents them from installing software. Finally, just in case, you should periodically completely reinstall your system from a fresh Fedora download (think of it as a great way to update your system while simultaneously ridding it of anything anyone might have sneaked in). How often you reinstall depends on how worried you are about someone messing with you. The more worried you are, the more often you should do a reinstall. Remember, Fedora is completely free to download, and only takes an hour or so to set up.

Hardware keyloggers are a little more tricky. I imagine they'd be harder to install on a laptop, because you'd have to partially disassemble the laptop and hide them inside it, but anything is possible. For PCs, keyloggers take the form of doctored keyboards (so sign the back of your keyboard with a sharpie to prevent it from being swapped out), or of little plugs that fit between the keyboard's plug and the PC's USB slot. You can check for anything weird or out of place, and if you find something you didn't install, take it down to the basement and crush it in a vice, or smash it with a hammer. Luckily, keyloggers are designed to be installed quickly by sneaky people in other people's houses, so you can usually find them if you look. Do a quick Google Image search for "hardware keylogger" so you can see what they look like.

OK, enough said about keyloggers... Back on topic, we're being very careful here. We're connecting over Tor, we're not using our real name, and we're encrypting our conversation. There's really no more secure way to have a conversation. As the Cryptocat developer notes, nothing is perfect, but we're getting pretty close at least. The screenshot on the next page shows what a Cryptocat chat looks like as it starts up (from here on in, I'm just going to show the Cryptocat screen itself, since it's the same on all systems).

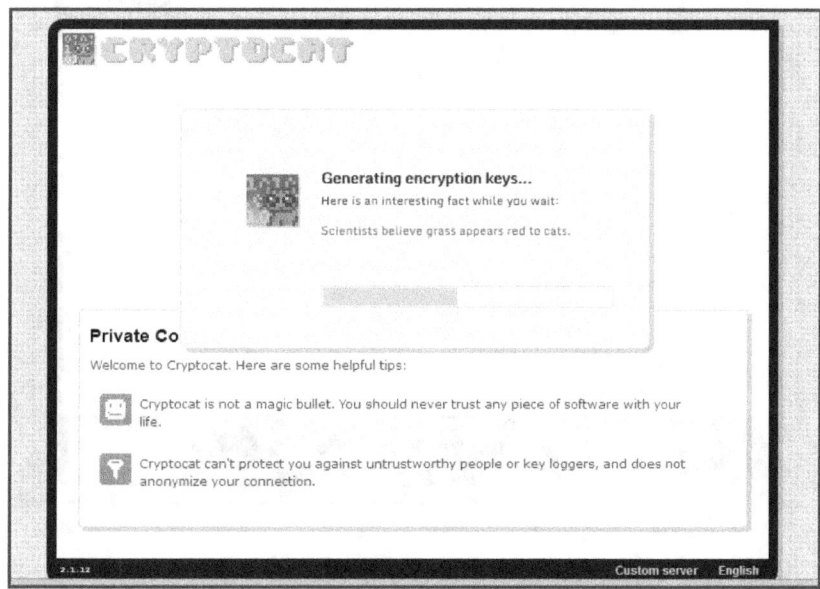

And here's what it looks like in progress. By the way, I'm logged in as another participant in a different Tor Browser tab, so we can see some actual action. Note that when the conversation first starts, it's a "group chat", and anyone who knows the chat name can join it. That's not secure, so you'll want to click on the other participant and start a private chat.

Here's the private chat that results when I click on "ILikeMyPrivacy2":

Note that it looks almost the same as a group chat, but now the "Conversation" tab is black and has a paw print in it. Also there are just the two of you. This is how you want to do things: nice and private. Type things in the text box, and click the blue button to send them.

Note that both group conversations and private conversations are encrypted. To find out more about a person you're conversing with, you can click the little downward arrow next to their name, and see some options. Available are "Send encrypted file", "Display Info", and "Block".

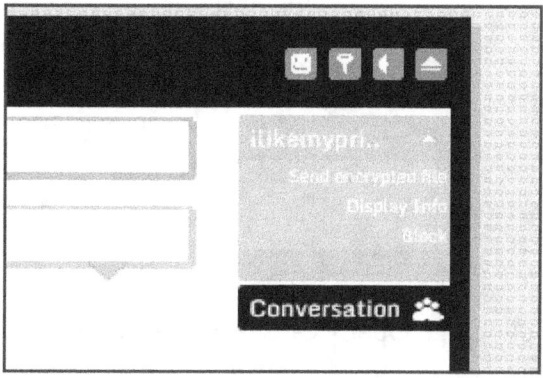

Sending an encrypted file lets you transfer files, obviously. Display Info lets you see some information about the encryption of the current conversation. Finally, Block lets you block a user who you don't trust, or who came in uninvited, or who you otherwise don't want to talk with. Let's send a file. Clicking that option brings up this chat window:

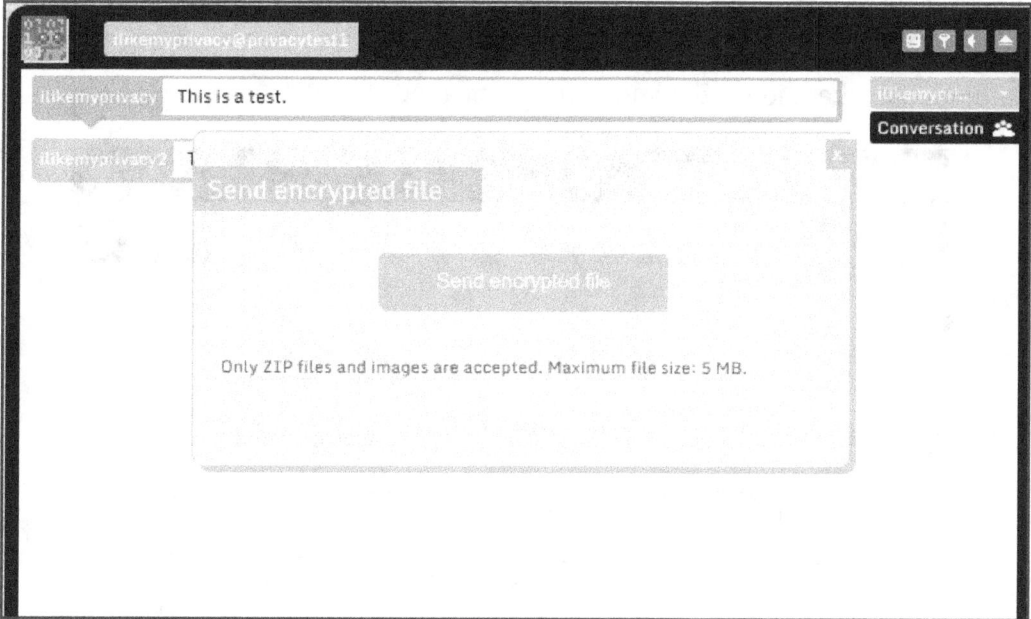

Let's send a zipfile from one particpant to the other, so you can see how it works. Here, we're back in a Gnu/Linux specific area, so I have to make some new screenshots. Let's click "Send encrypted file" in the above window, and see the "File Upload" window that results (note that you can only send images and zip files no larger than 5MB):

Protecting Your Privacy and Anonymity Online — Gnu/Linux Edition

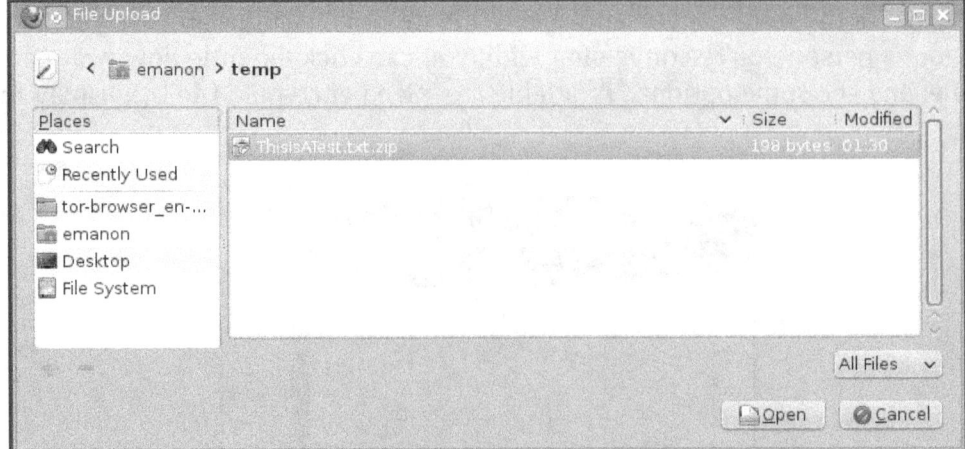

Selecting a file and clicking "Open" causes a brief progress bar to appear:

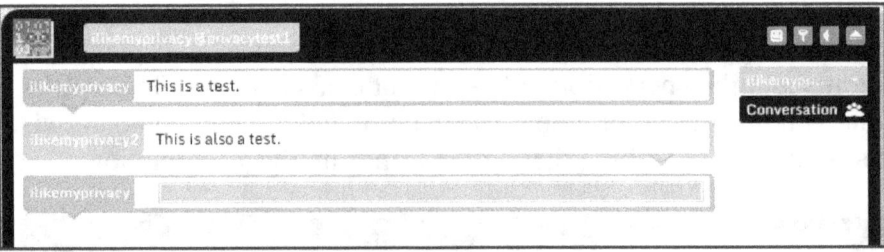

And, on the other side, a download link appears:

Clicking the download gets you the file. First, Tor complains:

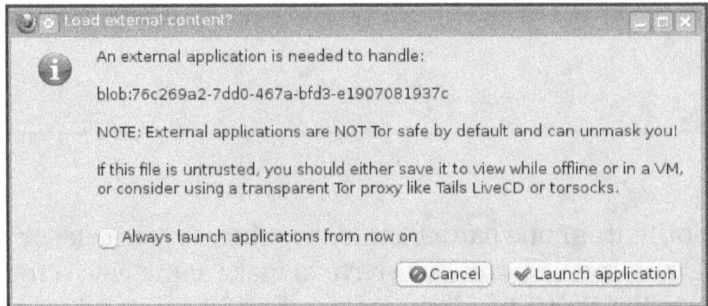

Don't check the box to always launch applications; you want to see these warnings, so

you don't do anything by accident that will wreck your anonymity. In this case, we know we're expecting to save a file so we'll allow it this time. Click "Launch application" and download the file:

I went and looked in the "temp" directory I saved to, and lo and behold, there it was, oddly named, but containing the test file I was expecting.

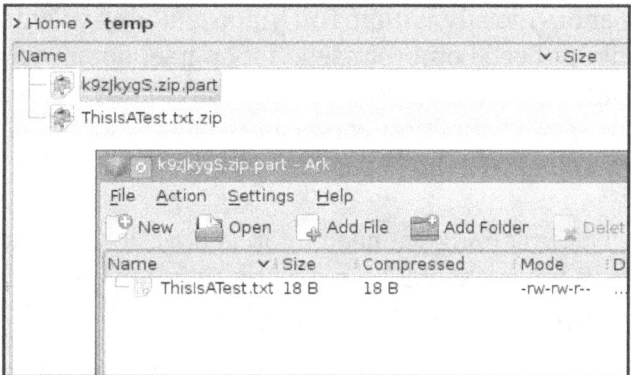

So that's Cryptocat. It's easy to use, totally works within Tor, and gives you a completely anonymous, encrypted channel for communicating with your friends. This is sufficient, of course, but we're not done yet. I'm all about options, you know, and I want to give you a second option which will let you communicate with people over *various different* protocols. Let's look at Pidgin, Gnu/Linux's powerful instant messaging client. As with everything else we've talked about, it comes with Gnu/Linux and can be downloaded right from the software repository (if you don't already have it).

Pidgin: A Rather Nice Instant Messaging Client
That Does Basically Everything You Need

Pidgin is a full-featured, very powerful instant messaging tool which offers Tor and Off The Record integration, for a fully anonymous, encrypted channel. The difference between Pidgin and Cryptocat is that you can use Pidgin with numerous instant messaging systems. Here, you're not communicating over an encrypted system being run by privacy activists, you're engaging in encrypted conversations using systems which normally aren't encrypted or private. In a sense, you're bending otherwise normal, non-secure, non-anonymous chat systems to your will, which is of course great fun.

Before we get started, a word of caution: You'll be using Pidgin with existing chat accounts, whether it's at Yahoo, Google, AOL, or some other provider. Assuming you want to encrypt your conversations, you also have to decide whether they have to be anonymous or not. If they have to be anonymous, you have to do some prep work: basically, you have to use the Tor Browser to set up an anonymous account as described in chapter 2. Remember the most basic rule of anonymity: an anonymous account has to be anonymous "from the cradle to the grave": you create it anonymously within Tor, you use it always with Tor, and you abandon it if you ever start to think it's been compromised. Of course, not all your conversations have to be anonymous. For conversations with your friends and family you can use any account you want, and supply any personal information you want to share. Just remember to keep your anonymous and non-anonymous activity separate.

Let's get started. The first thing we need to do is download and install Pidgin itself. Because you're using Gnu/Linux, it's available for you right in your Fedora software repository, as you can see here (I've selected both Pidgin and Off the Record for installation):

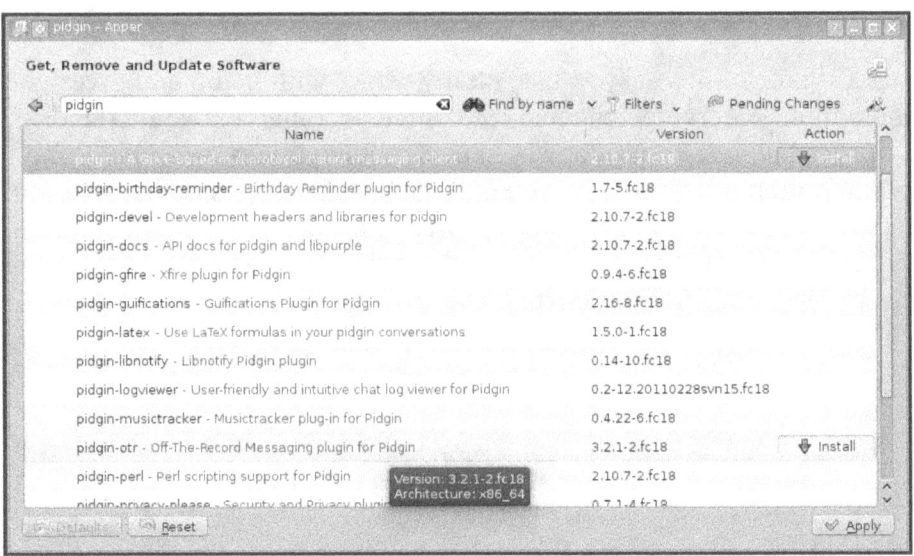

Once Pidgin is installed, you can find it in the main fedora menu, by clicking the round "F" button in the lower left hand corner. You can start Pidgin by clicking the "Applications" tab, then the "Internet" menu and finally Pidgin, as follows:

The Pidgin logo is a strange purple bird with a comic-style talk bubble over his head. When you start pidgin, it pops up a window telling you that you have no accounts set up yet, and inviting you to set one up:

Of course you'd like to set up an account, so you click "Add". For the rest of my examples, I'm going to use my "capitaldistrictgeek@programmer.net" account at mail.com, which can be used with AOL IM. Follow along, and set up your own accounts as per whatever providers you've got them with.

Protecting Your Privacy and Anonymity Online · Gnu/Linux Edition

First, notice that there are three tabs; here you can see the "Basic" tab, on which I've put in my account settings. On the left, you can see the tab and my settings; on the right, I've grabbed a picture of the protocols drop down so you can see how many different types of instant messaging Pidgin can handle (quite a few, extending way down out of the window).

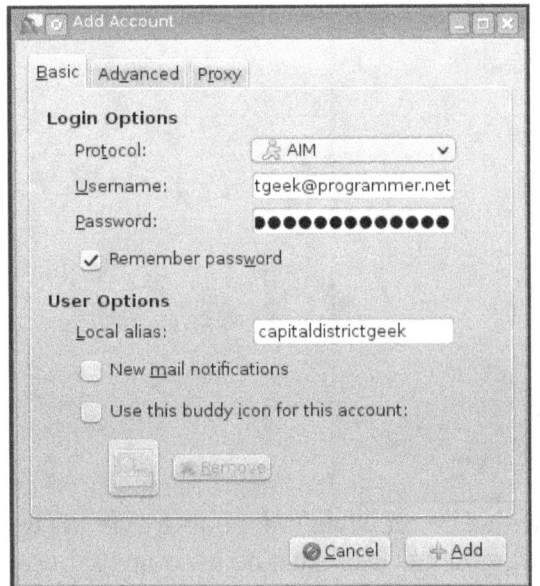
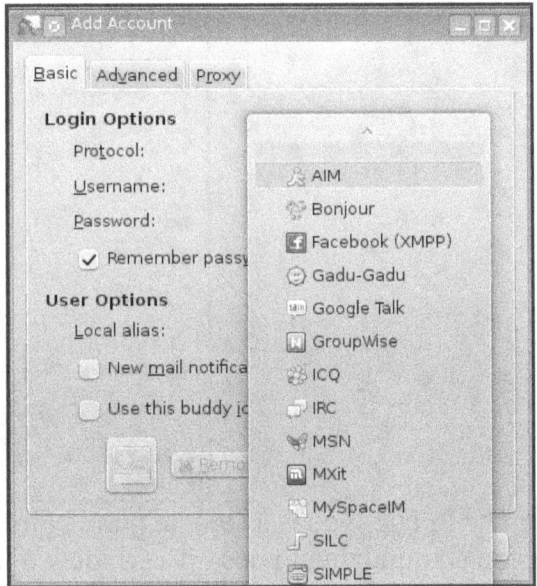

We don't have to do anything on the Advanced tab, but here it is for reference:

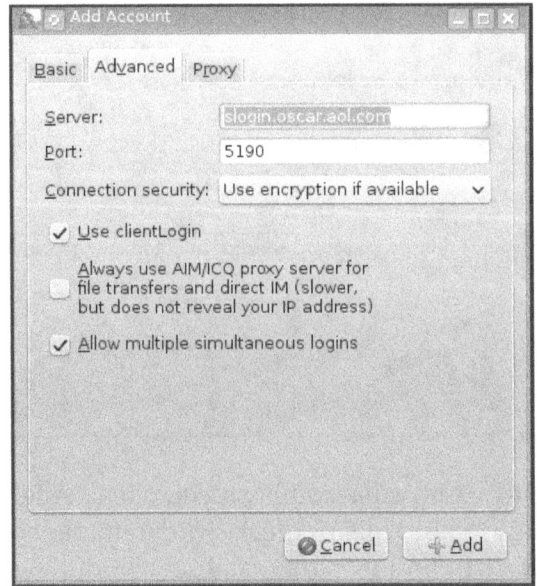

On the next page, we're going to see the "Proxy" tab, which we'll use to connect to Tor. Go ahead and click the "Proxy" tab, then go start Tor. If it's not running, this next part might not work very well, since the ports won't be open.

If you look at my "Proxy" tab, what I'm doing here is choosing the proxy type "Tor/Privacy (SOCKS5)". Then, I'm setting the host to localhost (127.0.0.1), and I'm setting the port to be 9150. I'm not setting a username or password yet.

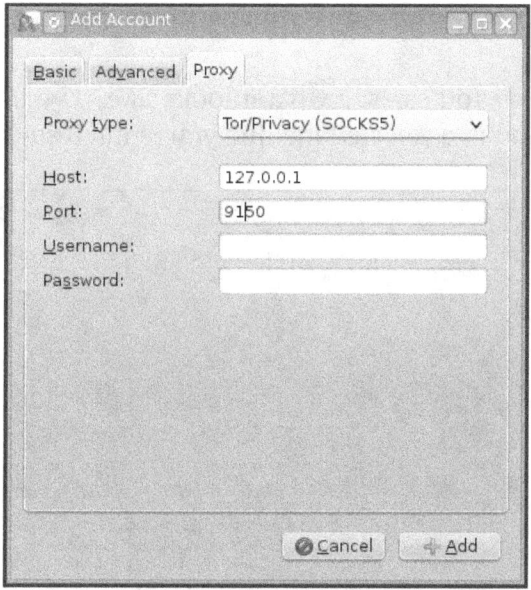

You're probably wondering, how do I know which port to use? Well, I'll tell you how to figure it out. First, switch to your Tor "Vidalia" window (the Tor control panel). Then, click "Message Log" as you can see here:

The message log window appears. Click the "Advanced" tab, as you can see below and look for a line like this one; the last two items in the log are the local IP address (127.0.0.1) and the port being offered so other applications can use Tor (9150).

Jul 28 22:36:09.274 [Notice] Opening Socks listener on 127.0.0.1:9150

Here's a screenshot, so you can see what it looks like. I've blurred out anything I'm not comfortable with sharing, and I've selected the line you're interested in...

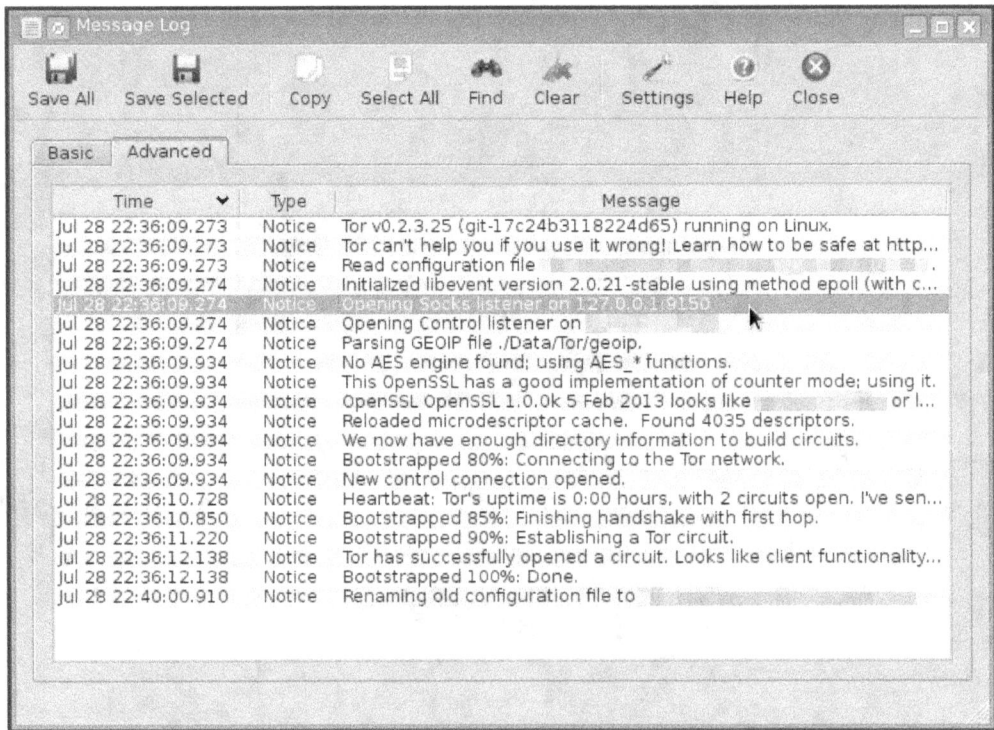

So, ok, we've set up our proxy info for Tor so we can use Tor with Pidgin, and we're done. Back in the "Add Account" window, click the "Add" button to add the account. Once the account is successfully set up, you should see this:

I made the window a bit smaller so the screenshot would fit, but I made sure all the text was visible. Your next step will be to enable the account you just set up. To do that, just click the Accounts menu, then "Enable Account", then your account, as you can see here (that's Niagara Falls in the background; my father took that photo in 1966):

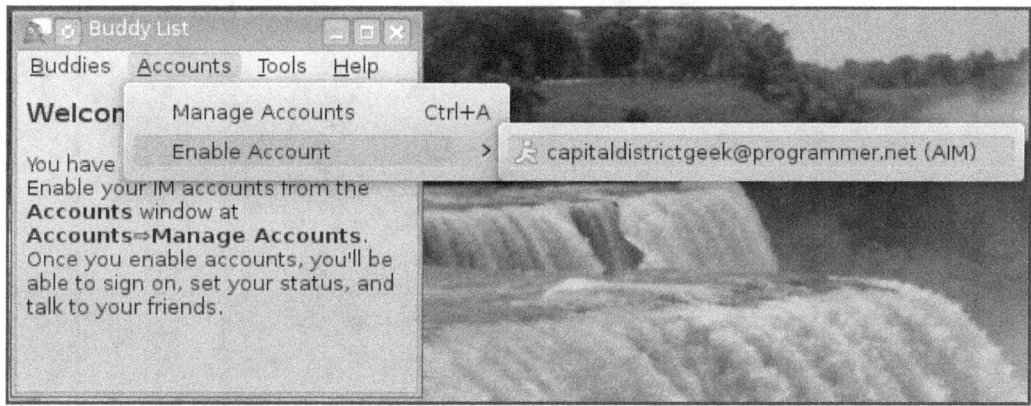

Once you enable the account, Pidgin's main window will change so it looks like the next image, and attempt to connect. Since we're proxying through Tor, if Pidgin successfully connects, that means you've got an anonymous Tor communications channel. Here, it shows me as "Available" so it was able to connect and we're ready to start communicating anonymously:

The next thing we're going to have to do is make sure Off the Record is configured and enabled. To do that, you'll have to click the "Tools" menu, then "Plugins", as you can see in the next image.

Here's the window that comes up. As you can see, I've checked the box to enable Off the Record Messaging, and I've selected it so you can see it better (the dark informational pop-up under it comes up when you mouse over it):

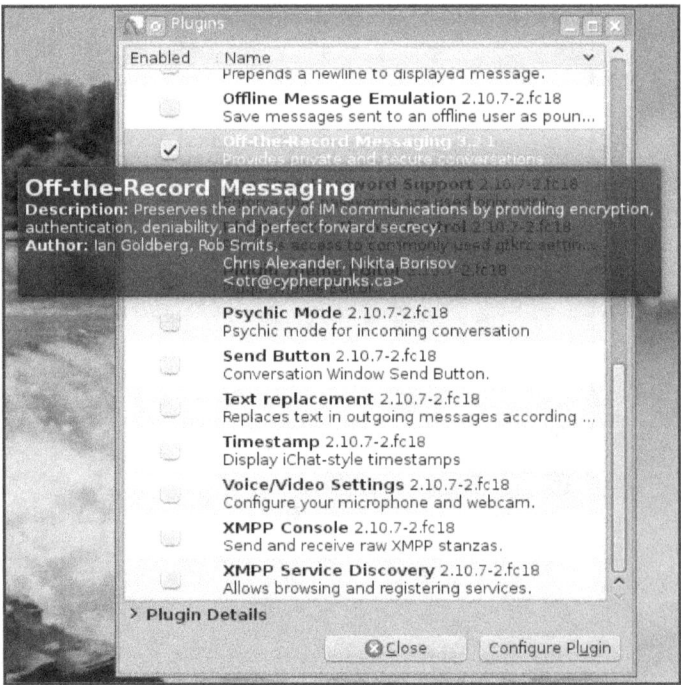

Now we want to configure Off the Record Messaging, so while OTR is selected (as in the above screenshot) click "Configure Plugin" to bring up the configuration tool. You should see the following:

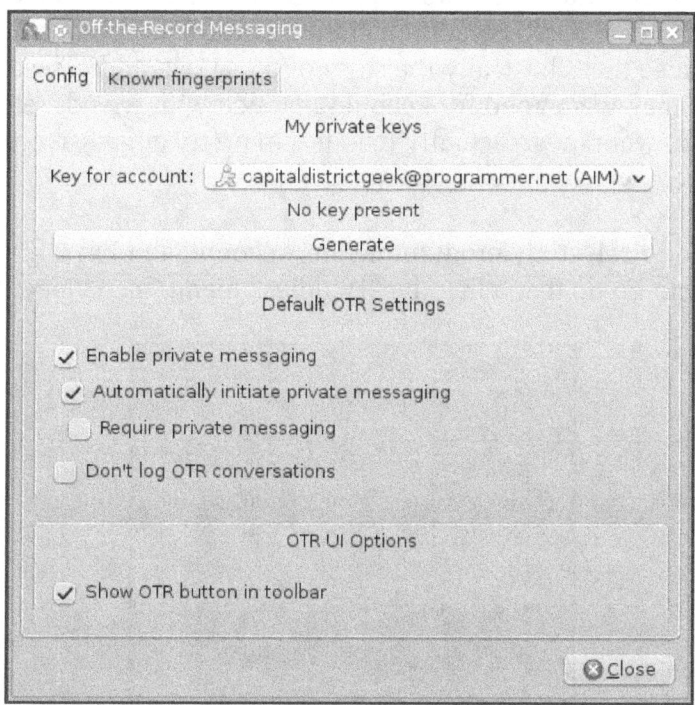

These defaults are actually pretty good. We want to be able to see an OTR button in the toolbar, we want to enable private messaging, we want to automatically initiate it, but we don't necessarily want to require it, and we don't want to log our conversations. Let's click "Generate" to generate a key for the currently selected account. While the key is being generated, we'll see a popup:

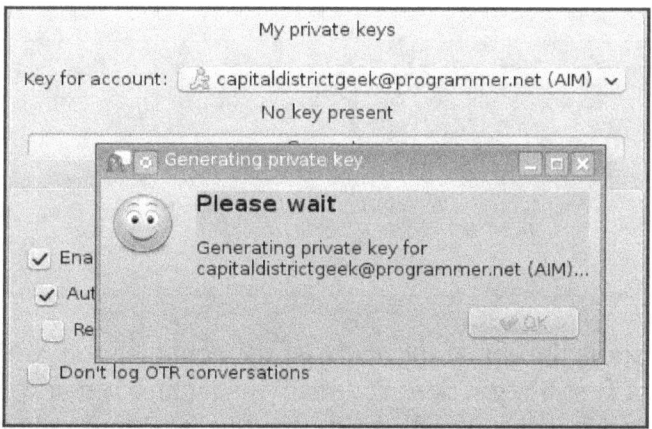

When it's finished, click "OK" and close out of the configuration window. Don't worry about the other tab yet, it just tells you about the keys of people you've chatted with.

OK, so it's time for us to try out some anonymous, encrypted chatting. For the purposes of the remaining examples in this chapter, I've set up two accounts in Pidgin, one for my capitaldistrictgeek@programmer.net email address, and one for my capitaldistrictgeek@techie.com email address. I used to work for the state government as a Java programmer and Oracle database administrator, and Albany is considered the "Capital District" of New York, so that's basically the story of those two addresses. They were only semi-anonymous, but they were good for keeping in touch with friends, etc. Don't send anything to them if you want me to actually read it; I'm pretty aggressive with the whitelist on those accounts. So, here we go.

First, I'm going to select my programmer.net account, and I'm going to start a chat with my techie.com account. To do that, click the "Buddies" menu, then "New Instant Message":

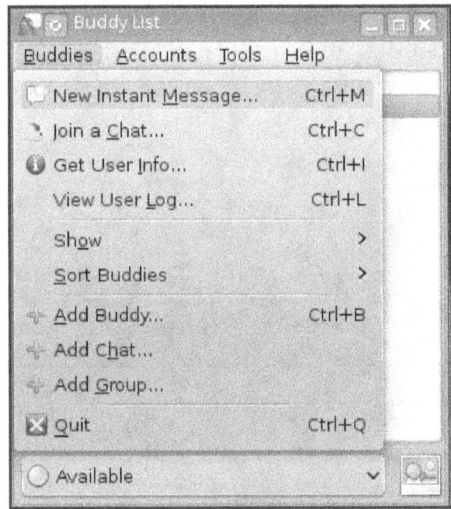

An instant message window appears, allowing me to select the account I want to use (the one at programmer.net), and who I'd like to communicate with (the one at techie.com).

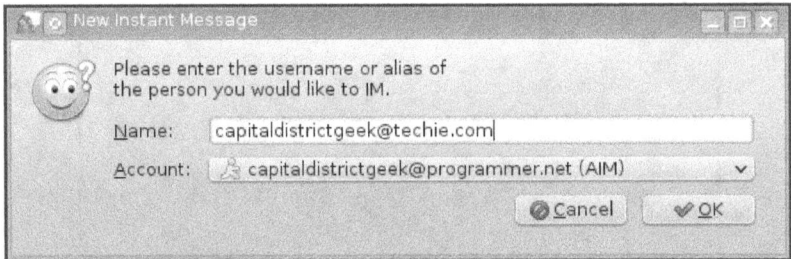

Clicking "OK" starts the actual instant message conversation, which you can see in the next image. Note that at first, Pidgin doesn't "trust" the techie.com account, so we can't have an encrypted conversation just yet. You'll notice that the OTR button in the lower right hand corner has red lettering, and says "Not private". Also, the green dot and account name shows *the person you're talking to, not your own account ID.* Here, we're going to be talking to capitaldistrictgeek@techie.com.

I'll send a text message to the techie.com account, saying "this is a test". Pidgin notices that there's a message waiting for the techie.com account, and opens up a new tab for me automatically. Now I've got one tab for techie and one tab for programmer; also in each tab, Pidgin and OTR reports that the conversation is with an "Unverified" partner and that the conversation is "Unverified" (the OTR button is now brown, not red, and right now, the conversation is already private, just not verified). *Again, the tab shows the name of the person you're talking to, not your name (so the first tab below is <u>from</u> programmer <u>to</u> techie):*

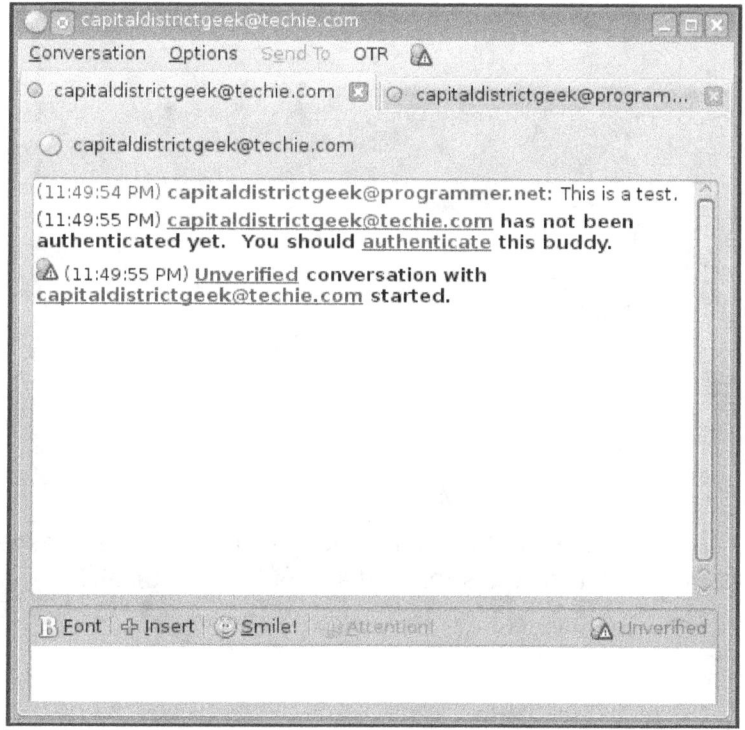

At this point, we've already got an anonymous, encrypted communications channel. We're conversing over Tor, and we're using Off The Record (OTR) for encryption, so we have "perfect forward secrecy" (nobody can go back to our conversation and try to decrypt it later on), So that's pretty good. But what's even BETTER is that we can use OTR to verify each other by asking a question only the other person would know. Or doing one of a couple of other things, but the question is the easier approach. You'd want to set this up in advance, by the way, maybe a set of questions and answers you agree on, and memorize, but never write down. So! As programmer, I try to verify techie. I click the OTR "Unverified" button, then "Authenticate buddy":

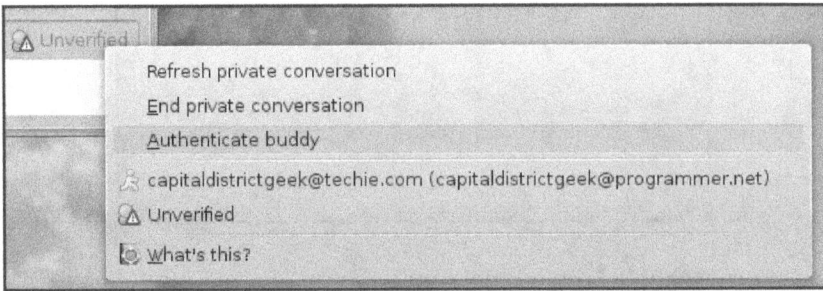

This brings up the Authentication screen, as you can see here:

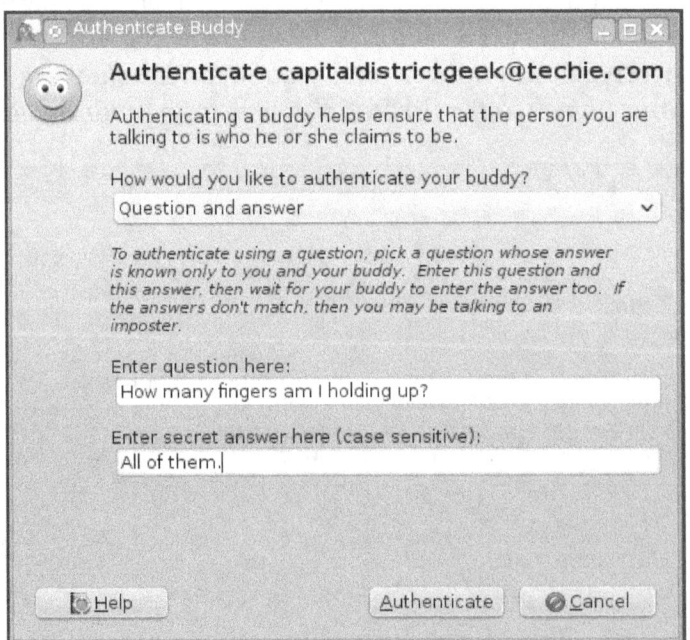

Clicking the "Authenticate" button sends the question and answer session off to programmer, who has to answer the question and authenticate himself.

Meanwhile, you see this window while you wait:

Here's the authentication window the other guy sees:

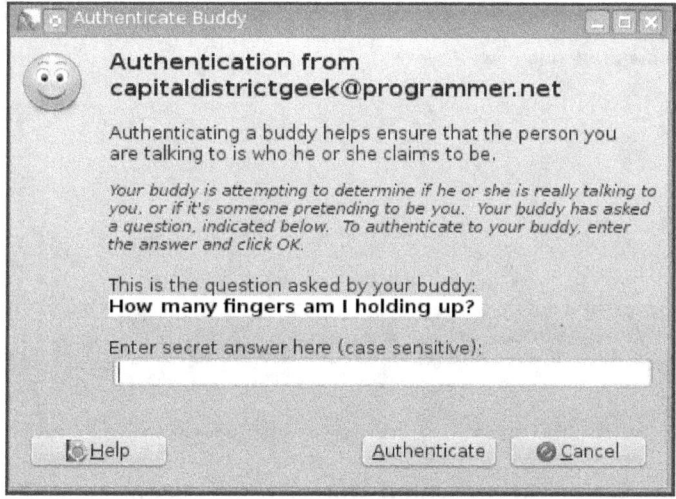

And when he correctly answers the question, you see the window on the left, and he sees the window on the right:

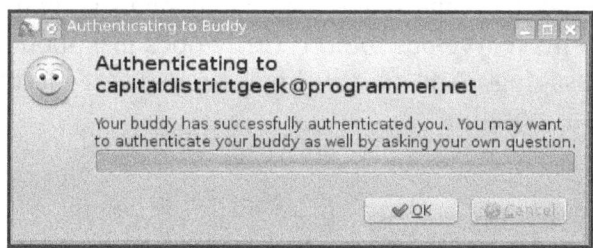

Note that Pidgin will suggest that your conversational partner should authenticate you as well, with a question and answer session of his own. This is only fair. I'll skip documenting that part, because it works exactly the same as what I've already shown you. However, I'll go ahead and authenticate back the other way, so Pidgin will show the conversation as being "Private" in both tabs.

Once you've both authenticated each other, your chat window will look like the following screenshot. Note that now the status of the conversation is "Private", and the OTR button text is green. You are now having a nice, confidential, encrypted conversation.

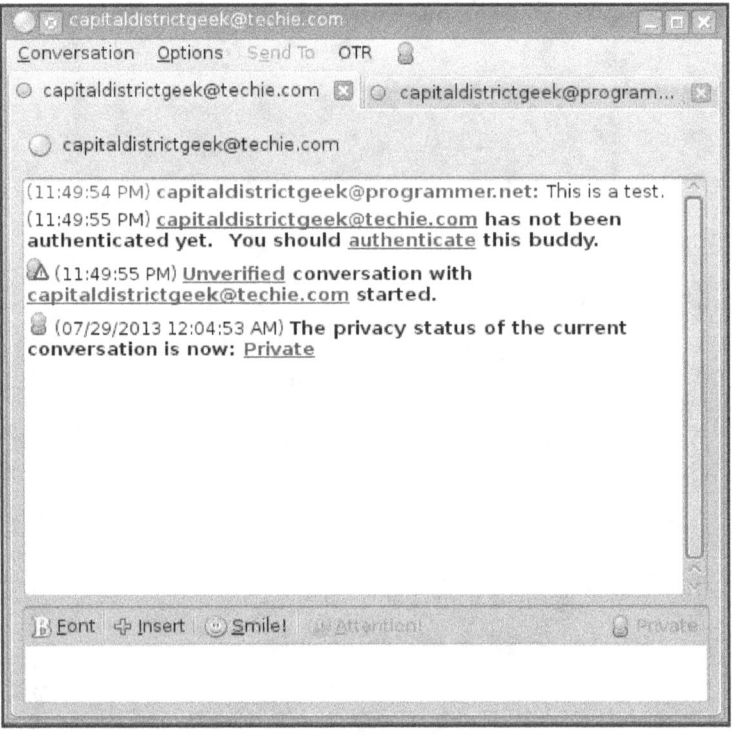

That pretty much wraps up encrypted, anonymous instant messaging, aka text messaging. Note that you can use Pidgin and OTR for every other text messaging protocol you want, including IRC. You are, as they say, "all tooled up".

Please go ahead and read the manuals so you get a fuller understanding of what you can do with this marvelous tool. It really does just about everything you can imagine related to text messaging. And now, we're done. All that's left to read are my final notes, which I'll keep as brief as possible.

Afterword:

And thus do I wrap up my Gnu/Linux edition of "Protecting Your Privacy and Anonymity Online"... This version is my favorite, because Gnu/Linux is my favorite operating system of all time. I like it even better than the BSD's, and I loved those. Working with it is a pleasure for me; it's an operating system by techies, for techies, and it feels like home.

You might have noticed that this version of my book is a bit shorter than the others. This is because everything you need is already available in the Fedora software repository, so you don't have to run around hunting for it. All you have to do is select it for installation and click an "Apply" button. No other operating system offers that kind of ease of use. It made my life quite a lot easier, believe me.

Now that the book is complete, all I have to do is upload the PDF to my website and roll out a paper version on Lulu (I want to buy some copies on paper... I like the feel of it, I'm old fashioned).

If you've bought this book on paper, thank you SO much. You're putting food on my table, and you have my gratitude. You might want to head over to my website, and download a PDF copy to put on your cell phone or tablet. It's FREE, and in full color. If you read the copyright page, you can see the permissions I've granted you to give copies of the PDF to all your friends, family, and coworkers, sharing it with everyone you can. Spread it around, get as many people as possible using Tor and encryption. It's good for us, and good for society. So please spread the word, and tell whoever you can about these free and open tools.

Again, the PDF can be found at http://tech-hermitage.com/PrivacyAndAnonymity/.

Thanks again,
Phil Perry
6/22/2014
11:00AM

www.ingramcontent.com/pod-product-compliance
Lightning Source LLC
Chambersburg PA
CBHW080919170526
45158CB00008B/2169